For Lucy, Ben, George and Wilfred

UNMITIGATED ENGLAND

Peter Ashley

Adelphi Publishers

The title *Unmitigated England* is from the first line of
John Betjeman's poem 'Great Central Railway
Sheffield Victoria to Banbury'
'Unmitigated England' / Came swinging down the line /
That day the February sun / Did crisp and crystal shine.
Betjeman put it in quotation marks because he in
turn is quoting Henry James, who used the phrase to
describe thatched roofs.

This edition
© Adelphi Publishers 2006
Text © Peter Ashley 2006
Images © Peter Ashley
unless otherwise stated

First published in 2006
by Adelphi Publishers
Northburgh House
10 Northburgh Street
London EC1V 0AT

Text by Peter Ashley
Design by Anikst Design LTD
and Peter Ashley
Edited by Sarah Peacock

ISBN 10: 1 84159 270 6
ISBN 13: 978 1 84159 270 1

Printed and bound in
Germany by Mohn Media
GmbH, Gütersloh

Sales information:
Random House UK
Tel. 020 7840 8463

Orders to:
Grantham Book Services
Tel. 01476 541 000

Frontispiece
Old Somerby church,
Lincolnshire

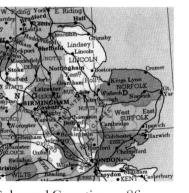

PREFACE

My dad, John Betjeman, would have loved this book, and I'm pleased it's being published in his centenary year. So many of his passions appear to be Peter Ashley's too: railway stations, churches, old-fashioned shops, the English seaside. And all those evocative household names– he would have particularly enjoyed seeing one of his own indulgences, a packet of Passing Clouds cigarettes.

But Peter Ashley ploughs a distinct and individual furrow. There's even one of his paintings here of a blue tractor doing just that in front of Happisburgh lighthouse. *Unmitigated England* isn't just another nostalgic *aide-mémoire*. It's a stylish wake-up call for us all to recognize again the small things that make England the England that we love.

The big landscape picture doesn't appear to change that much, but, when we get down to the detail so many of the images in this book remind us of what has gone. Whatever happened to those road signs that were so at home in the English countryside, so in scale with their surroundings? And why did British Telecom destroy nearly all our red telephone boxes in order to replace them with something so mediocre? The questions need to be addressed, and Peter has done a remarkable job in bringing them to our attention. Thank goodness he thinks to photograph so much of what is *real* England, away from the obvious, as he skilfully whittles out the neglected and the forgotten.

Of course these very English passions come in from the fields and lanes to rest on Peter's bookshelves. Having been brought up with the latest Shell Guides arriving with the postman (my dad created the Guides, wrote and co-wrote some of them, and edited all with his 'BF', best friend John Piper), I'm happy to see how groundbreaking and eclectic these books were. Particularly in the rare pre-war editions, over which my dad took such infinite care and chose all his favourite typefaces. Here was the England Peter cares so much about: country churches and chapels, architectural lettering, odd corners of remote towns. It's good, too, to be reminded here of the competition– Hugh

Casson's National Benzole books, a brand that appears to enjoy a number of walk-on parts in this book, and Clough and Amabel Williams-Ellis's Vision of England series.

Much has been written, photographed and painted on this book's subject. But here is a marvellously idiosyncratic addition to England's bibliography, from a champion who beats a very different drum in defence of his passions. Keep it to hand always, perhaps propped up between a Golden Syrup tin and a row of Shell Guides if you can find them.

Candida Lycett Green
September 2006

INTRODUCTION

[England] is somehow bound up with solid breakfasts and gloomy Sundays, smoky towns and winding roads, green fields and red pillarboxes. It has a flavour of its own. Moreover it is continuous, it stretches into the future and the past, there is something that persists, as in a living creature.

'The Lion and the Unicorn' George Orwell

opposite top
A short-lived 1930s' railway service: GWR stamp for air freight

opposite bottom
1936 LNER night travel leaflet

I haven't travelled very much outside England. I've spent a bit of time mucking about in France and Italy; I have drunk Ouzo on a rusty bucket of a boat listing between Corfu and Paxos (with a Fiat Strada strapped to the deck) but that's about it. Oh, and I once went to New York just to see a Rolling Stones concert. I think it's because from a very early age I realised just how much there was to see in England. For most of my childhood my father ferried us about by steam trains, and if we weren't sitting in sooty carriages then we were on the buses, clutching an Aldis projector and a screen. This was because we were often sent out into Leicestershire to show my missionary aunt's slides of Nigerian banana trees to audiences sitting open-mouthed in village chapels. And because my father had an eye for detail he gave a running commentary on everything we saw on our erratic passages. I couldn't get enough of it.

Ask any post-war boy or girl what a 1950s' childhood in England was like and the chances are they will stare into the distance and tell you

it was about as good as it gets. Odd really, considering that half the country was still scarred by war and the rest needed a jolly good coat of paint. Our Mars bars and KitKats were rationed, boys had to go about in short trousers even if they were sixteen and girls had side partings and ribbons in their hair. Everybody else had BO. But in between us all getting tuberculosis and having our tonsils out there was one almost subconscious pleasure. One we didn't really appreciate until we were either robbed of it or it simply disappeared. It's just that much of what we saw in our everyday lives actually *looked* rather good, and there was a definite sense of things also looking very different to each other, rather than all the same.

Perhaps there was a very elemental reason for this. The grotesque aberration of the First World War altered England forever. The 1920s and 30s then progressed at the pace of a Bentley Boy at Brooklands and the look of England changed up a gear. For the well-off, big-propellered aeroplanes roared up into the skies (some of them even taking off and

landing on water), express trains served cocktails as streamlined locomotives broke speed records, and characterful sports cars with enormous headlamps set off for the continent. A new middle class started hiking and buying houses in 'Metro-land', and everyone tuned into the BBC Home Service and bought Penguin Books.

Suddenly the premonitions of another war came horribly true and everything stopped. Although the Second World War only took up half of the 1940s, the rest of the decade was paralysed by deprivation, quite simply worn out. And that's why the early 50s were really the 30s– picking themselves up, dusting themselves off and starting all over again. So I went to school in a 1938 Leyland bus, the bread got delivered in a Jowett and the attic gave up a pre-war clockwork Hornby train set.

As soon as I was able to ride a bicycle without colliding with a gas lamp I was off. Everywhere I pedalled was still real countryside: village streets strewn with straw and spattered with beastly excretions; village churches always open, the vicars writing Sunday sermons in vast unheated vicarages next door. Village shops were stacked with

colourful cardboard and tin manifestations for
Tide, Monk and Glass custard and Rowntree's
Cocoa and were decorated outside with big
enamel advertising signs. Oxo came in red tins
we used for school lunch boxes, and scruffy
kids in hats still sniffed a gravy boat and said
'Ah! Bisto'. Newsagents sold us *Eagle, Girl, The
Beezer, School Friend,* and Dad his *Practical
Householder* and twenty Craven 'A'.

   On the road I avoided being run over by
bright yellow and black National Benzole
petrol tankers and duotone Hillman Minxes,
and back in school I stood transfixed in front
of Shell posters on the walls telling me about
moths and birds' eggs and faraway places with
names like Surrey and Middlesex.

above
Punch magazine for
15 April 1951, Festival of
Britain souvenir issue

right
Royal merchandise, a
transfer story book for the
Coronation

More English counties were discovered on holidays, when after weeks of mounting excitement we boarded express trains with black locomotives and carmine and cream – 'blood and custard' – carriages bound for Lincolnshire, or malachite green Southern electrics to Sussex and Kent. Midland Red coaches in convoy like a military exercise took a whole day to deliver us to Norfolk. And to top it all off we had the Festival of Britain in 1951, which showed us the new Penguin biscuit wrappers by Barnett Freedman and what it was like in outer space. Two years later we had a coronation that gave us everything from Union Jack periscopes to school parties where we got a free mug with the Queen on it. And the chance to watch it on a neighbour's brand new Ekco television.

So, is all this just self-indulgent nostalgia from a splenetic old git trying desperately to crawl back to the halcyon days of a secure and sunny childhood? Probably. But I hope that this book will demonstrate more than that. Of course *Unmitigated England* is about a vanished world, a comfort blanket to hold up against the tyrannies of the new century, but it's also a record of my discoveries of what we've managed to keep: beautiful landscapes and buildings, familiar brands, surviving detail. Most of all it's about the *visual* appeal of England, of what we've lost and how we are in constant danger of losing even more. Not just because it's old or quaint, but rather because we increasingly have to suffer decision makers with absolutely no sense or appreciation of just what it is that gives England its unique identity, and as a result can't wait to destroy it in order to swamp us with tawdry, mediocre replacements.

right

S.J. Moreland made
England's Glory matches
in Gloucester from 1891
until Bryant & May closed
the factory in 1976.
Ironically England's Glory
are now made by the
Swedish Match Company
in Tidaholm, Sweden. The
Ship is HMS *Devastation*

opposite

A very English car in a
very English town: an
open-topped Bentley
tourer in Great Malvern,
Worcestershire

It isn't that I don't like the age I now live in.
I'm glad I don't have to live in fear of catching
typhoid, I quite like the Gherkin building and
really like the new Bentley Continental, even
though spitting footballers buy it. But my work
continually pulls me back into the past. I've

taken pictures ever since I had a camera that
wouldn't let light in, but over the last ten years
I have photographed in literally every corner
of England. I've combined a selection of these
images with the odd painting and with items
from my scrapbooks and collections of
packaging and ephemera. Emptying out my
drawers, one might say. It will, I hope, show
that we did indeed reach a high point in those
less cynical, less material early post-war days.
My choices are very personal, somewhat

arbitrary and tend to lean towards the English
countryside and its coastal margins. After all
it's rural England that's most under threat. But
there is still much to enjoy out there. As
Captain Nolan says of it all – newly-arrived
from foreign climes in the opening scene of
Tony Richardson's film *Charge of the Light
Brigade* –, 'It is good. England is looking well.'

MARMITE ON OUR HOVIS

Humourist Alan Coren once wrote for his column in *The Times* a riposte to John Major's odd plea for us all to 'get back to basics'. Coren asked what these basics were and presented a homely scene that relied on brand names to evoke a pastiche of a perfect past. It involved a dutiful wife filling the *Ideal* boiler with *Coalite* whilst hubbie polished the *Morris Eight* before smoking a *Park Drive* over his *Reader's Digest Condensed Book*. *Express Dairies*, *Wincarnis*, *Monk and Glass custard* and *Cherry Blossom* were amongst a roll call of evocative brand names summoned up to complete an idealised portrait of post-war domestic bliss.

Many iconic brands have now either disappeared or have been so radically exploited and done over by the dead hand of marketing that they no longer have anything like the same appeal. As I write, the New Jersey (*sic*) owners of Oxo and other household names are booting up to kick the brand out just because it doesn't make the millions quick enough. Their UK man said, 'Our portfolio in the UK and Ireland includes some strong brands but it is highly fragmented [bit like an Oxo cube] and has not met our growth expectations. It is time to explore strategic alternatives.'

But what is it that makes us think comfortably about certain brands and not others? Is it that they exude a certain Englishness, even when, like Ovaltine, the origins are in Switzerland? Quite simply, there are some brands that really do punch an emotive weight far above their intrinsic value as basic commodities, and it is as much to do with the visual appeal of their packaging as it is the ingredients hiding within. Our responses to them are borne out of a familiarity that no marketing department can ever hope to emulate in a month of focus group meetings.

BIRD'S
CUSTARD

He gives his Ovaltine a stir
And nibbles at a "petit beurre"

'The Wykehamist', John Betjeman

Ovaltine

Ovaltine was originally a malt extract drink invented in Berne in 1865 by Dr George Wander, but its story really came to life in England when his son Albert founded A.Wander Limited in the village of Kings Langley in Hertfordshire in 1909. The countryside location was considered vital for very sound reasons. Not only was the factory sited in close proximity to main roads and farmland supplying the basic ingredients of barley, milk and eggs, it was also next to the

Grand Junction Canal (now the Grand Union).

This 'Home of Good Health' developed in the late 1920s with a new Art Deco building, designed by managing director Harry Hague, and the famous Ovaltine farms. Up at Abbots Langley, Parsonage Farm was rebuilt as the Dairy Farm in an almost rural Disney-esque style with half-timbering and thatched roofs to house the pedigree herd of Jersey cows. Numbers Farm, nearer the factory, was re-created in a fairy-tale horseshoe shape to become the Poultry Farm.

And so, the Ovaltine barges set off along the canal as the wireless sets of England warmed up so that the nation's children could sing along with The Ovaltineys on Radio Luxembourg: 'At games and sports we're more than keen; / no merrier children could be seen, / because we all drink Ovaltine, / we're happy girls and boys.'

A vanished world. We don't say 'keen' and 'merry' much these days, and games and sports can no longer be synonymous with happy children because we might upset those who can't run very fast.

Gone, along with Ovaltine's presence in Kings Langley. I suspect the canal trade went first, the barges loading up one more time at the Grand Union wharves. The farms quickly followed; the Dairy Farm now an exclusive over-priced housing development, the Poultry Farm restored after years of dereliction to house a wind turbine office. (There's a sales sample sticking up next to it; look out for both between junctions 20 and 21 on the M25.) The fabulously-fronted factory was unexpectedly closed in 2002 with the loss of 245 jobs and production moved back to Switzerland. The last I heard it was being made back in England somewhere, with the ingredients doubtless being shipped in by motorway from industrial farms hundreds of miles away. Remember how it was: a local factory employing a local workforce in the countryside, using raw materials grown and gathered within yards of the production line to create a product taken away by canal barges. And think of the Dairy Maid finally setting her basket of barley and eggs down in the pantry, slipping off her Bobby Shaftoe shoes and putting her feet up with a well-earned mug of Ovaltine.

The lamplight shone upon this gutter, and he observed a torn piece of newspaper lying in it – a headline of the Western Gazette *– and just tilted against the edge of this headline he saw an empty greenish-coloured tin … 'Lyle's Golden Syrup'… Much sweetness had he, in his time, watched Gerda imbibing from such a greenish-coloured receptacle!*

Wolf Solent, John Cowper Powys

Lyle's Golden Syrup

Reading *Wolf Solent* is a bit like wading through Golden Syrup. The Victorians first put a green and gold tin of it on their tables in 1882. It was a teatime essential in my boyhood that will forever be associated with Jim Laker taking nineteen Australian wickets in a test match at Old Trafford in 1956 (ten of them in the second innings); and a recently-emptied steel can is in front of me now holding pens and brushes. With their snug-fitting lids they also make excellent spider-removal units if you happen to live with an arachnophobe. After decades of countless spoons dipping into the gloriously viscous liquid the can design has hardly changed, even after the Lyles amalgamated with their Silvertown neighbours and competitors the Tates to form Tate & Lyle in 1921. Always with the curious engraving of a dead lion hosting honey bees alongside a fragment of Biblical text from the book of Judges: 'Out of the strong came forth sweetness'.

above
The virtually unchanged Lyle's Golden Syrup can

right
Rare Golden Syrup promotion, a recipe book that includes one for 'Half Pay Pudding'

Colman's Mustard

Tate & Lyle tankers still swing out of the Silvertown refinery on the eastern reaches of the Thames and Colman's still mill mustard as yellow as their tins at Carrow on the south side of Norwich. Mustard seeds from Norfolk acres for a brand so English it was perceived as the essential condiment, presented in silver pots on country house dining tables and slotted in next to plates and cutlery in robust wicker

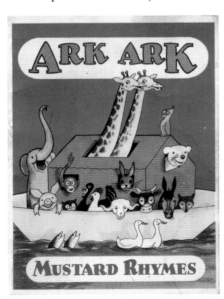

above
A balancing act from Colman's book of *Mustard Rhymes*

right
Mustard Rhymes book

far right
Colman's Mustard tin

picnic baskets. Their advertising became legendary, from big vitreous enamel signs in yellow and dark blue to mustard pots, mirrors, wall charts, a Mustard Club and little books of nursery rhymes for children: 'Some little pigs are cool as ice, / Some little pigs get flustered; / But when it comes to dinner-time, / All little pigs need mustard.' Bring on the bacon sandwiches. And remember, never accept mustard in one of those dreadful sachets that squirts it all over your fingers.

Oxo

Oxo's origins are similar to those of Marmite, with German chemist Justus Leibig perfecting a concentrated extract of beef in the nineteenth century, but it was the English who took it to heart as a sustaining drink sold as Oxo at station buffets, race courses and agricultural shows. They say the name may have come from the letters O-X-O being chalked by a docker on a crate of the extract to distinguish it from others on a quayside, but I think the 'Ox' part is a bit of a give-away. So familiar was the simple logo, the architect A.W. Moore got around advertising restrictions in 1928 by making the windows of Oxo's new warehouse tower on the South Bank in London the same shape as the letters. Like Marmite and Colman's, Oxo entered an English advertising vernacular with innovative and humourous posters, like the painting of an Oxo cube sitting surreally on an aircraft wing with the slogan 'On a Plane by Itself'. For George VI's Coronation in 1936 Oxo sold six cubes in a beautifully-made tin money box with a souvenir leaflet. And who can forget Katie and her television family, remarkably all sitting down together for an Oxo-enlivened roast?

above
1936 Oxo money box for the Coronation

top right
Oxo cookery book c. 1935

bottom right
A pre-war Oxo cut-out tin figure used for slipping under packets on grocers' shelves

Shredded Wheat

Shredded Wheat so loved their spanking new Welwyn Garden City factory they put a stylised illustration of their works on the box. At one time they even tacked 'Welgar' in front of the brand name. Later, health-giving properties were extolled by a boy dressed-up in a Lifeguard's uniform. Louis de Soisson designed the factory in 1925, one of the landmark buildings in the brave new world of garden cities started earlier in Letchworth. Its refreshingly open location gave it room to breathe, an aspect that can still be admired today from trains passing between King's Cross and the North. Compare it withHorlick's red-brick colossus in Slough (a copy of the company's Wisconsin factory), which looks as if it's making gear boxes. The Shredded Wheat factory is how food manufacturers should look, white and eau-de-nil silos and easy-clean metal windows, all looking as hygienically wipe-down as a kitchen surface. Long may it be here, a factory unashamed to be seen as just that, not hidden away on an industrial estate, and with the added bonus of looking like a confident expression of the brand. It makes me want to eat three at a time.

Hovis

right
The once familiar 'Teas
with Hovis' sign

below
The green and gold
'V'-shaped sign, seen here
in Eastfield Road,
Peterborough

Smith's Patent Germ Flour was patented in 1887 by its inventor Richard 'Stoney' Smith, a miller from Stone in Staffordshire, and Thomas Fitton, from nearby Macclesfield. Smith was so enthusiastic and successful in the selling of his flour that Fitton bought the Imperial Mills next to the House of Lords on a site now occupied by the Victoria Tower Gardens. Millbank takes its name from a succession of mills here on the bank of the River Thames. Fitton and Smith realised that a snappier title for their wheatgerm flour was desirable, and held a national competition to find a brand name. It was so very nearly Yum Yum, but thankfully the winner was London student Herbert Grime with Hovis, a derivation from the Latin *hominis vis*, meaning 'the strength of man'. This is why Hovis once had a punctuation mark (a tilde in fact) over the 'o', to denote the foreshortening. On his death Grime's widow was paid a pension by the company. The name has flourished, not just raised on the side of loaves but on the walls of countless bakeries and shops, either with cut-out wooden letters or the more familiar 'V'-signs jutting out in green and gold. Sets of these signs were kept in the prop stores at all the major film studios, no English village street scene was complete without one.

John Bull

Out on the road teashops using Hovis were supplied with wooden signs bearing the legend 'Teas with Hovis', and the stern adjuncts 'The Rule of the Road' or 'The Highway to

ed area, rubber solution and the essential strip of pink patches. There was also a blue chalk sprinkler with a little rubber stopper and some surgical looking material I could never fathom

Health'. Did those cyclists pulling up for cold tongue sandwiches also have a John Bull repair outfit in their saddlebags? Vital for mending punctures, the smart tin was bright blue with an embossed John Bull in his Union Flag waistcoat assuring us that the equipment was 'made for the man who will have the best'. Inside was a yellow crayon for marking the location of the puncture, sandpaper for scrubbing the infect-

out and hoped I'd never have to use. The tin also told you the whole lot was made in England (at the Evington Valley Mills in Leicester) and that if you'd fitted John Bull tyres in the first place you would 'have practically no use for this outfit'. Dunlop's tin had an embossed base to facilitate the grating of the chalk, next to the text 'Dunlop Accessories for the Wise Man's Tool Kit'.

above
Edward Young's Penguin trademark

right and opposite
The Penguin grid was ideal for colour coding: orange for fiction, blue for biography, green for crime, red for plays, magenta for travel and yellow for titles that didn't fit anywhere else. An odd purple stood in for essays and *belles-lettres*, and a pale blue was used for the now defunct (and sadly missed) Pelican Books

Penguin Books

It all looked so good, the branding of England. By the mid-1930s we were almost subconsciously surrounding ourselves in a comfort zone of familiarity. As dark and supremely evil forces abroad screamed gross distortions of a pseudo-mythological past to turn mindless bigots into brown-shirted thugs, we invented Penguin Books.

Edward Young. An early meeting tells of the embryo staff trying to think of what to call the books and, recalling previous paperbacks imprinted with an albatross, were writing down names of seabirds. A secretary typing away behind a partition joined in by shouting out 'penguin', and they all looked at each other in relief. Young was dispatched to London Zoo

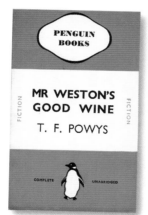
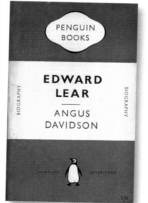

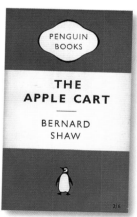

In 1935 Allen Lane well and truly upset the publishing apple cart by bringing out cheap paperback versions of titles hitherto only available in much more expensive hardbacks. The immediate success of the slim volumes was due in no small measure to the design, originally conceived by Lane's production manager

and the first manifestation of the penguin was drawn. Matched up with the very *moderne* orange banding for fiction and Eric Gill's utilitarian typefaces the brand was born.

Their pocketability was also a vital factor in their phenomenal popularity. Station bookstalls kept them for railway passengers, they fitted into hiking knapsacks and the armed forces preparing to defend us against those Teutonic bullies stuffed them into their kit bags. They became as essential an item of kit as tin hats and khaki webbing. Many soldiers went to war with the Penguin editions of Adrian Bell's country trilogy – *Corduroy*, *Silver Ley* and *The Cherry Tree* –, constant reminders of the England wait-

Penguin celebrate their seventieth anniversary the original iconic design is perhaps even more popular, not only on very collectable books but equally as a device plundered to grace everything from drinking mugs to deckchairs. Best of all, there are now some wonderful new covers appearing that once again follow the Penguin tradition for ground-breaking design.

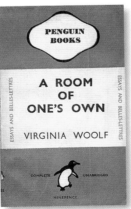

ing for their return, an England about to change irrevocably, never to be the same again. Post war, the design gradually evolved to include illustrations and then, after a heyday of innovative covers that were hallmarks of book design, they became just like every other paperback. Market forces took over, but as

Dinky Toys

right
Dinky Toy postman

below
The Dinky Supertoy
Regent petrol tanker and
the Dinky Toy Riley saloon

Post-war England also saw bright yellow boxes appearing in toyshops that were a literally brilliant antidote to the deprivations of wartime and its intendent rationing.

Dinky Toys had, along with the other superb products of Binns Road in Liverpool (Hornby trains, Meccano construction sets), been around since the 1920s. Toy cars, vans and lorries were sold out of yellow stapled boxes that held a quantity of each model, but the 50s saw what was probably their golden age. Diecast renderings of popular road vehicles, each came

in its own box with a picture of the particular model on two sides. Larger, more expensive models were called Dinky Supertoys and were encased in blue and white striped boxes. Stacked up in toyshop displays they were not only a superb visual treat but their bright new paintwork collectively gave off a smell that will still make those of a certain age go very misty-eyed just at the memory. The commercial vehicles were probably the most appealing; the Royal Mail van in post-office red and the GPO telephone service van in a deep bronze-green with its silver roof ladder were exceptionally desirable. But it was those familiar brands again that brought us colourful liveries: A Morris J for Capstan cigarettes (just imagine), Bedfords for Ovaltine and Kodak, Austins for Nestlé's and Raleigh Cycles and those curious but utterly unique Trojan vans for Oxo, Dunlop, Brooke Bond Tea and, best of all, Cydrax in mid-green with its scrumptious apple and yellow lettering. Supertoys gave us Guy lorries for Ever Ready batteries, Spratts dog biscuits with the pictogram Scottie logo wagging its tail and the

airbrushed full colour on the back cover. Inside we quickly skimmed past the monochrome photographs of hydroelectric dams in places like Tanganyika to reach the centre spread where the new vehicles were shown in action in plywood dioramas. Commer breakdown trucks towing Standard Vanguards (in at least three colours) down cardboard dual carriageways, AA patrolmen struggling with their sidecars in cotton wool snow. Every issue had at least one photograph of a collector who made us all jealous by the sheer quantity of his Dinky Toys, drawn up in serried ranks on a neatly trimmed lawn (cut by an Atco, obviously). Invariably there would be a child in big shorts blinking into the colonial sun of some far-flung outpost of the Empire.

Suddenly it was all over. The competition set in with Corgi Toys ('the ones with windows') and Spot-On from Triang; the neat boxes stopped, replaced by acetate-fronted all-purpose cartons that were themselves heralds of the appalling blister packs that followed. In fact everything changed. Dinky Toys were replaced in our loyalties by the Beatles' first Parlophone singles, the *Meccano Magazine* by the *New Musical Express*. I suppose we all grew up. Almost.

heart-stopping Golden Shred with the much-maligned golly clutching his jar of marmalade. I still have my most treasured holiday purchase, the Foden Regent petrol tanker bought for fourteen shillings and sixpence from a Great Yarmouth shop in 1955.

We looked out for new models in the monthly *Meccano Magazine*, presented in

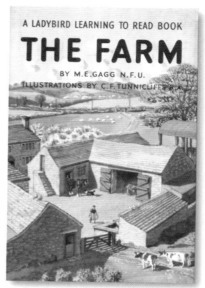
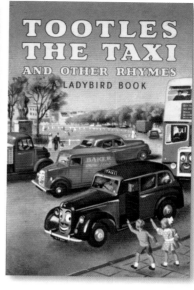

Ladybird Books

Richard the Lion Heart in a St George tunic takes on the Saracens in a Palestinian desert; John and Susan go with Mummy to the greengrocer, chemist and ironmonger, whilst purple loosestrife and greater stitchwort grow by a shady stream. A postman in red striped trousers empties a pillar box into his GPO Mini Van; pigs, sheep, horses and five ducklings live in peaceful coexistence down on the farm and Colin the cattle truck takes them all to the abattoir. Welcome to the pocket-sized world of Ladybird Books.

The format was simple; each book $4^5/_8$in by 7in, with around twenty-five spreads divided between stunning full-page colour illustrations opposite pages of unambiguous text, set in a classic, legible typeface. Between 1940 and 1980 Wills & Hepworth in Loughborough

published over a thousand titles, but aficionados will tell you that the best of them stopped in 1975. The earliest were nursery tales, titles that would now empty John and Susan's Mummy's purse several times over, but it's with the educational series that Ladybirds made their biggest impression. How many children today could pull themselves away from their PlayStations in order to do an experiment from *Magnets, Bulbs and Batteries* or make and fly a kite using *Air, Wind and Flight*? The Ministry of Defence used *Understanding Maps* to teach basic orienteering skills and I still use *The Ladybird Book of Trees* above all other arborial guides. A collection of original Ladybird Books goes far beyond completist shelf filling; treat them as pocket handbooks to guide you around another world. And always wear sensible shoes when you read them.

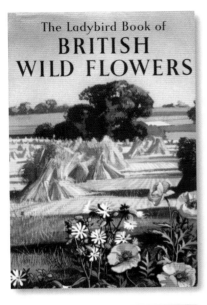

The Ladybird Book of
BRITISH WILD FLOWERS

RICHARD THE LION HEART

A LADYBIRD BOOK

An Adventure from History

A LADYBIRD LEARNING TO READ BOOK

SHOPPING WITH MOTHER

TEXT BY M.E. GAGG N.F.U.

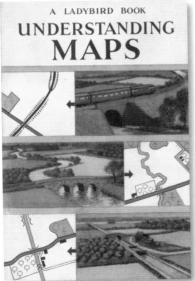

A LADYBIRD BOOK

UNDERSTANDING MAPS

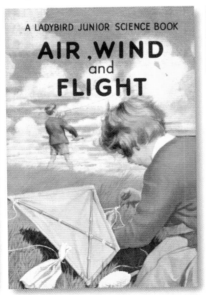

A LADYBIRD JUNIOR SCIENCE BOOK

AIR, WIND and FLIGHT

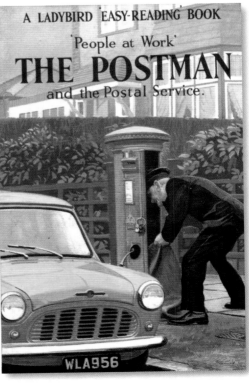

A LADYBIRD EASY-READING BOOK

'People at Work'

THE POSTMAN and the Postal Service.

WLA956

Mr Therm

In the early 1930s the Gas Light and Coke Company needed something simple to put on their vans and advertisements so they employed illustrator Eric Fraser to design a symbol. He came up with an absolute classic– Mr Therm, a cartoon flame that presented a warm, comforting image to bring a little levity to an austere public service. Fraser received £5 for his trouble and, after negotiation, a further £25 for all subsequent usages. Mr Therm's career survived well into the 1960s, gracing the communications of what were now regional gas boards. It was all so straightforward then. Gas came into your home, the Gas Board sent you a bill, you paid it and they kept sending you more gas. If you smelt gas there was probably a leak and a gasman came to fix it. And if you wanted a new cooker or boiler they were very enterprising and had gas showrooms where you went to see what was on offer.

There's still something named British Gas, which it isn't really because it has to be called 'Scottish Gas' in Scotland and 'Nwy Prydain' in Wales. There isn't an 'English' Gas and it's owned by a company called Centrica who don't mind what anything is called so long as it makes lots of money and can be dealt with by a call centre. They bought the AA once. You can buy gas from the electric people now of course, and we really won't be surprised when Tesco sell it alongside the frozen Chicken Tonites. But rest assured Mr Therm will have nothing to do with it.

Marmite

top right
Marmite centenary label

centre right
Marmite cubes tin

bottom right
Marmite cookery book.
One of the '100 ways'
of using Marmite is in a
savoury nourishing
custard especially
formulated for invalids

Old brown Marmite jars must be the most ubiquitous glass containers unearthed by the collector digging for bottles. Love it or hate it, as they say, the familiar Marmite jar has been a pantry staple since 1902 when the Marmite Food Extract Company was born in Burton-on-Trent in Staffordshire, centre of a brewing industry that provided Marmite's essential ingredient of yeast by-product. The name comes from the French for 'stewpot', an example of which still graces the label, and Marmite retains its appeal not just from the essential teatime spreadings on soldiers of bread but also for its jar shape and label. Originally sold in earthenware pots, the glass jar first appeared in 1928, and I remember when the closure was once a fascinating metal clip that sprang off and threatened to amputate your fingers, now replaced by the yellow plastic cap.

CHURCHMAN'S

Special **Nº 1** Special

CIGARETTES

W. A. & A. C. CHURCHMAN,
IPSWICH & NORWICH.

CLIFTON

SPECIAL CUT

Cigarettes

Turkish

PLAYER'S

ANCHOR

CIGARETTES

TIPPED

"WILD WOODBINE"

RED LABEL

W. D. & H. O. WILLS,
BRISTOL & LONDON.

SENIOR SERVICE
The Perfection of Cigarette Luxury

FULL STRENGTH

CAPSTAN

Navy Cut

CIGARETTES

W. D. & H. O. WILLS

HIGNETT'S

Golden Butterfly

20 CIGARETTES
FINEST QUALITY.

TRAWLER

Navy Cut

CIGARETTES

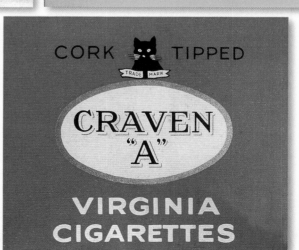

CORK TIPPED

TRADE MARK

CRAVEN "A"

VIRGINIA
CIGARETTES

PLAYER'S
"WEIGHTS"
THE ORIGINAL
Made from
PURE
VIRGINIA
TOBACCO

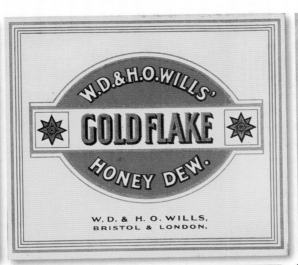

W.D.&H.O.WILLS'
GOLD FLAKE
HONEY DEW.
W.D. & H.O. WILLS,
BRISTOL & LONDON.

"PASSING CLOUDS"
20   20
Cigarettes.
W.D. & H.O. WILLS.

Paymaster
EXPORT

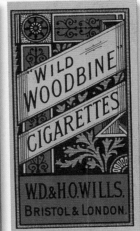

WILD
WOODBINE
CIGARETTES
W.D.&H.O.WILLS.
BRISTOL & LONDON.

PLAYER'S
NAVY CUT
HERO
REGD Nº 154011.
CIGARETTES
"MEDIUM"

OUR BELIEF, THE FINEST LEAF

Kensitas
CIGARETTES
FILTER TIP

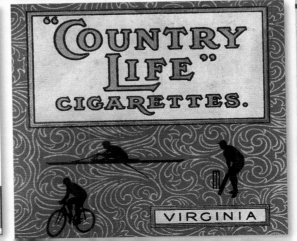

"COUNTRY
LIFE"
CIGARETTES.
VIRGINIA

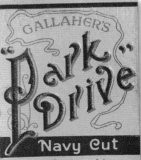

GALLAHER'S
"Park
Drive"
Navy Cut
Manufactured by
GALLAHER LIMITED.
VIRGINIA HOUSE
LONDON & BELFAST.

C

WILL'S
CIGARETTES.

WILLS'S CIGARETTES

POTTING YOUNG PLANTS

Cigarettes

I no longer smoke cigarettes. Not because of some hectoring government directive and certainly not as a result of being confronted by their propaganda, which takes up half the surface area of my occasional packet of twenty Capstan. No, it simply wasn't doing me any good, as anyone who smokes is fully aware without distorted half-truths being rammed down their nicotine-ravaged throats by ASH (Action on Smoking and Health). ASH self-righteously claims it isn't against smokers and talks in 'mission statements' with headings like 'Our Vision'. As Iain Sinclair says, always beware of anyone other than a poet having a vision.

Gone are the days when we could enjoy a Player's behind the bike shed, a Churchman's No.1 in the greenhouse or a Gold Flake in a hospital bed. Gone the pleasure of finding cigarette card 'Garden Hint No. 10: Making a Plant Propagating Frame' in our Woodbines or the final coupon for a Teasmade in our Kensitas. Smoking has been turned into a subversive activity, soon to be banned in its natural home, the public house. How long before the Tobacco Police storm publishers' offices to remove books with references to cigarette brands in them? Domino telling James Bond of her schoolgirl hero on the Player's packet blue-pencilled from Ian Fleming's *Thunderball*; Betjeman's line – '*Coco-nut smell of the broom, and a packet of Weights / Press'd in the sand…*' – expunged from 'Pot Pourri from a Surrey Garden'.

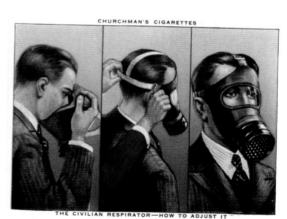

CHURCHMAN'S CIGARETTES

THE CIVILIAN RESPIRATOR—HOW TO ADJUST IT

left and above
Art in the packets: cigarette cards from Wills's Signalling and Garden Hints series and Churchman's Air Raid Precautions

opposite
Vitreous enamel signs for various brands, a rambler's notebook, playing card backs, Wills's Woodbine tin cricket game

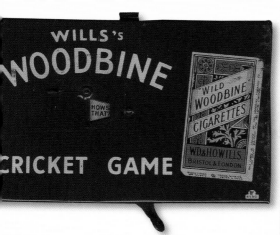

WILLS'S WOODBINE CRICKET GAME

WILD WOODBINE CIGARETTES

THE "GREYS" 10 CIGARETTES SILK CUT VIRGINIA CIGARETTES 20 for 1/- 6d "GREYS" ARE GREAT!

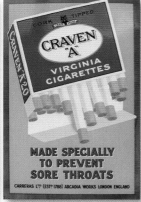

CORK TIPPED CRAVEN "A" VIRGINIA CIGARETTES MADE SPECIALLY TO PREVENT SORE THROATS CARRERAS LTD (EST? 1788) ARCADIA WORKS LONDON ENGLAND

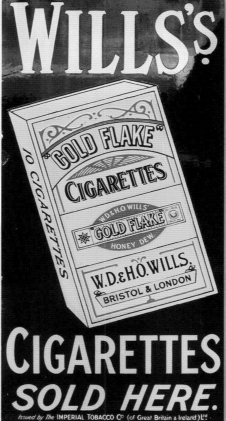

WILLS'S "GOLD FLAKE" CIGARETTES 10 CIGARETTES W.D.&H.O.WILLS GOLD FLAKE HONEY DEW W.D.&H.O.WILLS BRISTOL & LONDON CIGARETTES SOLD HERE. Issued by The IMPERIAL TOBACCO Cº (of Great Britain & Ireland) Lᵗᵈ

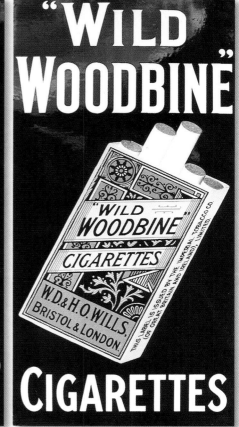

"WILD WOODBINE" "WILD WOODBINE" CIGARETTES W.D.&H.O.WILLS. BRISTOL & LONDON. CIGARETTES

H.M.S.EXCELLENT Player's Please

WILLS'S WOODBINES

WILLS'S GOLD FLAKE For Quality

WHEREVER YOU GO Wills's Gold Flake Satisfy TRADE MARK N E W S RAMBLER'S NOTE BOOK

SONGS OF PRAISE

opposite

Stanley Badmin's front
cover illustration for the
Easter issue of the *Radio
Times* (18 April 1954)

If you were brought up in the mid-twentieth century then you will almost certainly recognise S.R. Badmin's meticulous and didactic work from books like *Trees in Britain* and *Village and Town* in the Puffin Picture Books series and, of course, in *The Ladybird Book of Trees*. In fact no one drew trees quite as well as Mr Badmin. His Easter cover for the *Radio Times* (opposite), although in black and white, is full of implied colour and impeccably drawn detail. Through the bare elms with their attendant rooks can be glimpsed a road descending through folds of downland to a village street lined with blossoming trees. A bowler-hatted shepherd with a lamb under his arm coaxes his flock towards the bridge, where early swallows swoop under the arches past celandines and pussy willow.

The most telling detail comes as the eye is drawn into the shadows of the lych-gate, where this bucolic scene is being observed by a lady and, presumably, her daughter as they pause on the steps, carrying baskets of spring flowers which you know are about to be artfully arranged around the lectern and on the window sills of the church. One also knows that the Easter services, for which their careful decorations will act as a scented backdrop, will

'worship the Lord in the beauty of holiness', as the hymn goes. Familiar and well-loved sentences from the 1662 *Book of Common Prayer* rather than mediocre bullet points from an Order of Service which reads like a manual for a microwave oven. And the congregation will also worship in the security of knowing that the vicar won't get everyone hugging each other or, even worse, suddenly whip his guitar out.

Places of worship have always been very personal for me. I was brought up a Strict Baptist, which meant chapel three times on a Sunday, frightening apocalyptic sermons and, even more nerve-racking, baptism by total immersion in a heated white-tiled pool in the basement. It had a lot to do with my maternal grandfather being the pastor of the Wellingborough Tabernacle, a huge pale brick chapel in the side street of a small Northamptonshire boot-and-shoe town. Not being takers of drink the congregation avoided talking about the fact that the whole forbidding edifice had been paid for by local brewers.

So chapels always came first. Red-brick Nonconformism up in the Chilterns, at urban crossroads and out in remote Norfolk cornfields– we became Primitive Methodists on holiday for some reason.

right
A social cup of tea in
the branded crockery
of the Tabernacle
in Wellingborough,
Northamptonshire

below
1916 postcard of the chapel

But there were always the country churches, destinations for my earliest cycle rides with a bottle of Tizer in the saddlebag, developing a passion that now means my own family feel obliged never to go out of their front doors without one of Pevsner's guides under their arms. With the help of these Buildings of England books and the idiosyncratic Shell Guides (q.v.) I learnt the difference between Perpendicular and Decorated, started to know my predellas from my pulpitums and what those knobbly bits are that stick out of church spires

(crockets). With John Betjeman's help in both his poetry and his unsurpassed introduction to his *Collins Guide to English Parish Churches* I also learnt to look beyond architecture.

I never get tired of that first lifting of the latch in the porch, the echo still resonating as I step down into the chill interior. If it's somewhat neglected there may be the smell of mouse-nibbled hassocks and musty hymn books; if it's well cared for there will be the heady scents of furniture polish and flower arrangements of the Constance Spry School. Always a quick look behind heavy curtains screening off the tower to see if there are bell ropes looped-up above mops and buckets and unused oil lanterns covered in a patina of ancient dust. Standing in silence to catch the heavy click of a clock or the ratcheting of a bell about to strike. Brass memorials in the main aisle (contributions for

The Tabernacle and Pastor's House, Wellingborough.

above
Winter idyll on the River Nene at Cotterstock, Northamptonshire

rubbings gratefully received) may have been replaced by over-zealous Victorian restoration with encaustic Pugin-style floor tiles, but the hand-painted numbers on the doors of wooden box pews will probably still be visible. There may be a medieval tomb chest with a knight and his lady in hand-clasped sleep – '… faithfulness in effigy… ' as Larkin put it in 'An Arundel Tomb' – , their feet on family pets, children gathered around the base. Plain window glass will distort churchyard yews, coloured glass will make rainbows on the chancel steps. Brass-eagled lecterns will hold catering-size Bibles and wooden Gothic hymn boards will hold last Sunday's playlist from *Hymns Ancient & Modern*.

My England journeys have caused me to lift the latch in hundreds of churches, maybe even a thousand. None have really disappointed; there's always been something to catch the eye, something to make me think. But equally there are many that have left deeper and more lasting impressions.

First Outings

My first expeditions were out into High Leicestershire, essentially the east of the county, where it rises up in undulating hills until it runs into the limestone belt in Rutland. Cranoe with its back to a steep hill topped with rook-haunted trees (Cranoe: hill of crows, indeed), Gaulby with its curious Chinese pinnacles and then, just round the corner, Kings Norton. It was here that my passion for churches had the blue touch paper well and truly lit. This is an extremely early example of the Gothic revival, a 1760 design by John Wing. Approaching the tiny village across hedge-lined pastures the church dominates the landscape, perched high above its precipitous graveyard. You make your entrance by climbing steep

High Leicestershire
Churches

opposite top left
St John Baptist, Kings
Norton

**opposite bottom right
and below**
St Michael, Cranoe

opposite bottom left
St Peter, Gaulby

*Once I am sure there's nothing going on
I step inside, letting the door thud shut.
Another church: matting, seats, and stone,
And little books; sprawlings of flowers, cut
For Sunday…*

'Church Going', Philip Larkin

steps up to the front door in the tower, and on pushing it open the breath gets taken away by the untouched interior. The clear glass in the east window shows the red-brick farmhouse next door, and light floods in on the original box pews and a three-decker pulpit sitting right in the middle of the nave. Across the west end a gallery sits on fluted columns. It's the austerity that impresses, the spare workmanlike finishes that one probably expects from a more dissenting style.

St John Baptist, Inglesham

Hot and Cold Interiors

top left

Bell rope in Southwick
church, Northamptonshire

top right

Inglesham in Wiltshire
with Jacobean box pews
and a Perpendicular
quatre-foiled font

Inglesham in Wiltshire is a more recent discovery. Down a lane off the busy Swindon to Lechlade road the tiny church of St John Baptist sits near the Thames with only farm buildings and a manor house for company. I came here on the recommendation of a friend ('What do you mean you've never seen Inglesham?') in driving rain with a strong westerly wind blowing. My spirits lifted as soon as I entered the south door.

I actually wanted to shout for joy and in fact I think I did. Inglesham is Late Norman and Early English with fragments of pink and madder-coloured wall paintings, texts in medieval black letter, Elizabethan box pews and a Jacobean pulpit. Nothing appears to have changed here for centuries.

We have William Morris to thank for that. Over at nearby Kelmscott he heard that the church was about to be restored and knowing what this would doubtless entail he offered his services. Everyone expected a completely new church after the latest fashion, but Morris utilised great skill and craftsmanship to simply repair what was rotten or damaged. This was in 1888–89, a landmark piece of conservation by the Society for the Protection of Ancient Buildings, which Morris had founded. I sat in a box pew as the wind howled around the church and made the door rattle on its iron hinges, thinking of Morris loudly giving instructions and waving his arms about.

St Mary Magdalene, Tixover

The village of Tixover in Rutland has moved away over the centuries and left its Norman church alone in the meadows by the River Welland. You need to get the key from one of the cottages just off the main road and walk across a field, but it's worth it. That unique chronicler of the English landscape W.G. Hoskins wrote in his *Shell Guide to Rutland* (q.v.), in an appendix called 'Time Off in Rutland', 'I have found Tixover churchyard a pleasant place for an afternoon doze'. I did this one hot summer afternoon whilst photographing a little book on Rutland that used text from Hoskins's guide.

I was expecting two friends to join me and on waking up I staggered off into the church. On looking out through a window I saw two people approaching the porch, their figures distorted by the ancient glass. I don't know to this day what made me do it but I went and hid behind the big curtain that closed off the tower and, on hearing them enter, I jumped out with a blood-curdling scream. Of course it wasn't the expected friends and I spent the next twenty minutes calming down an hysterical woman. When my pals arrived a few moments later they quite rightly asked what on earth I was doing.

opposite

Fotheringhay church on
the banks of the River
Nene

bottom

The magnificent
sixteenth-century pulpit
in Fotheringhay church,
Northamptonshire

St Mary and All Saints, Fotheringhay

In his book *O More Than Happy Countryman* H.E. Bates called St Mary and All Saints in Fotheringhay, 'a superb church standing like a small lost cathedral over the graves of kings'. It also stands above the River Nene as it winds through what Bates called 'green pudding country', negotiating its last meanders before crossing the Fens to The Wash. Fotheringhay's royal connections are manifold, Elizabeth I erecting monuments to Yorkist Dukes in 1573

(the corpse of one of them returning here having being 'smouldered to death' at Agincourt) and, fourteen years later, signing off the bloody execution of her cousin Mary, Queen of Scots at Fotheringhay Castle.

This is a magnificent fifteenth-century church, the proportions slightly odd owing to the removal of the chancel, also in 1573. The eye continually wants to put it back, but what's left more than compensates. Flying buttresses curve up in support of the nave, the square tower turns into an octagonal lantern sprouting battlements and pinnacles until everything is topped out with the Yorkist badge, a gilded falcon and fetterlock.

With all this going on outside one might expect the interior to be a bit of a let-down. It isn't. Broad aisles, box pews and superbly-lettered monuments let into the floor are reasons enough for lifting the latch, but the centrepiece is the stunning, beautifully-painted and intricately-carved pulpit, a gift from Edward VI. The visual impact of a clergyman preaching from it must be like one of those medieval illuminated paintings where abbots motioning a two-fingered blessing lean disproportionately out of highly-coloured pinnacled buildings.

East Guldeford, East Sussex

Lowick, Northamptonshire

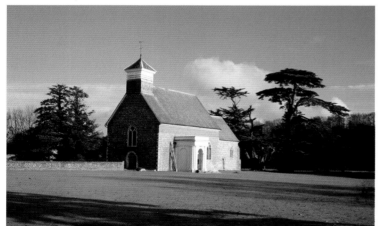

Lullingstone, Kent

Shelton, Norfolk

Batcombe, Dorset

Stanway, Gloucestershire

...ngham, Essex

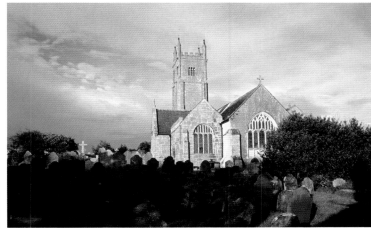

Ugborough, Devon

...dington, Cambridgeshire

Hallaton, Leicestershire

...nodoc, Cornwall

Exton, Rutland

above
St Peter-on-the-Wall, out on the Dengie Peninsular, Essex

opposite left
The chapel interior

opposite right
Wild flowers on the field edges along the approach to the chapel

St Peter-on-the-Wall, Bradwell

The creeks and inlets of the Essex coast have always held a particular fascination for me. So near to London, but so remote, the tidal estuaries create landscapes of airy isolation to the east of the last urban fringes. Between the Rivers Crouch and Blackwater the Dengie Peninsular is crossed by a handful of secondary roads and that rare thing, a branch railway, which finally gives up at Southminster. Beyond Tillingham and Bradwell-on-Sea the last lane peters out, and it's here you must leave your car and walk the last half mile down a track towards the horizontal line of the sea that is only punctuated by what appears to be a big farm barn. Indeed up until the 1920s this is exactly what it was.

The Romans were early inhabitants of these bleak margins, their fort of Othona guarding the eastern approaches; the Saxons followed with a settlement built for much the same purpose. All of it now gone beneath the waves or absorbed into the coastal mud. Except for the Saxons' place of worship, a truly remarkable Essex landmark built on the Romans' wall and recycled from the same brick and stone, founded by a missionary from the north, St Cedd. It survived demolition in later ages owing to its convenience as a seamark for shipping; a happy state of affairs that led to its use as a barn

and, later, the rediscovery of the chapel, one of
the earliest in England. The dedication is now to
St Peter-on-the-Wall, and the cool, dark interior
is a place of great solace and comfort if one walks
here alone in the heat of summer through the
poppy- and cranesbill-edged wheatfields. The
openings made for agriculture can still be
discerned in the exterior fabric, but inside
simple wooden benches are now arranged where
wagons and reaping machines were once stored
in the gloom with only the birds twittering up in
the roof to break the silence.

All Saints, Brockhampton-by-Ross

opposite top

Brockhampton-by-Ross:
Arts and Crafts vernacular
in deepest Herefordshire

Church Peripherals

**opposite bottom from
left**

Open half-door in the
Porch at Brooklands, Kent
Owston churchyard,
Leicestershire
Noticeboard at Butley,
Suffolk

All Saints at Brockhampton-by-Ross in Herefordshire is the Church of England in a somehow comforting pipe-and-slippers frame of
mind; an almost agricultural vernacular
enlivened with very sophisticated touches,
realised by local craftsmen and perfectly suited
to its deeply rural location. This is an Arts and
Crafts masterpiece by William Richard
Lethaby, built in 1901–02 in a simply stunning
amalgam of local sandstone, weatherboarding,
wooden shingles and very domestic thatching
over, amazingly, concrete. Peter Davey in his
Arts and Crafts Architecture places it amongst the
great monuments of the movement, noting as
well that the nave windows have 'clear leaded
panes, so that if the sermon is dull, the congregation can look out onto God's creation'.
Slightly distorted trees moving silently against
a Sunday sky. They could just as easily be dis-
tracted by the Burne Jones tapestries or the
choir stalls carved in a riot of bluebells and
buttercups.

Sadly, Lethaby got into trouble over All
Saints by insisting on being master builder as
well as architect. If escalating costs weren't
enough, which he felt obliged to meet out of
his own pocket, the very foundations started to

Royalty at prayer

left
The prayer book for the 1911
coronation of George V

above
Quintessential Quinton:
A Salmon postcard of
Sandringham church
in Norfolk from a
watercolour by A.R.
Quinton (1853–1934)

shift. It all proved too much, and the little
Herefordshire church was his last work. He
spent the rest of his life writing and teaching,
dying in 1931. One of his friends said of him,
'… he was about the jolliest companion
anybody could dream of, always full of life.' This
Herefordshire church is a perfect memorial.

St George Reforne, Isle of Portland

opposite
St George Reforne, Isle
of Portland, Dorset,
photographed by
John Piper

The Isle of Portland is shaped like a dewdrop about to fall from Dorset's coastal nose. The coastline is rugged and dangerous, shelves of underwater rocks under the beam of the red and white striped lighthouse at the Bill, cliffs still indented with quaysides where wooden derricks slung blocks of stone down into ships. At the centre of it all is the solitary and marvellously eccentric church of St George Reforne, west of the village of Easton and of course built in Portland ashlar.

I find enormous appeal in eighteenth-century churches. This was the age of architects with names rather than anonymous stonemasons, and the rules had started to be bent if not broken. Hawksmoor, whose influence can be seen here, is a prime example, designing and building extraordinary churches in the wake of Wren's post-fire London. And this is exactly what I like about St George Reforne; it's as though it was built for a city and, at the last minute, abandoned here on a blasted Dorset hill top. Erected on the very edge of its quarry this is the one that didn't get away, unlike all those Wren and Hawksmoor churches that had their birth in Portland quarries, their individual stones cut and fashioned here before embarking on their sea

journeys to London. Odd to think of all those domes, columns and volutes emerging from this landscape, fresh air replacing stone, the reverse of Rachel Whiteread's *House* sculpture. H.V. Morton came here in 1927 and a quarry foreman pointed to a long gash in the rock and casually told Morton it was the Cenotaph.

Local mason Thomas Gilbert designed the church – built between 1754 and 1766 – and put in all the oddities and fads of his age. The domestic pediments remind one of Aynho church in Northamptonshire, a tower with Tuscan columns and a finialled cupola, a curious dome over the crossing of nave and transepts and, inside, galleries, box pews and twin pulpits.

St George Reforne also has a sense of place unique to its location. The graveyard is immense, a veritable forest of tombs and monuments leaning starkly against the sky. Here is a Georgian and Victorian extravaganza of death, skulls and angel wings presiding over the ranks of Portland's dead and over those not intending to be here at all, the shipwrecked who were cast up on the barren shores. A place for ghosts certainly, even on the brightest of days.

ENGLAND ON FILM

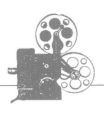

The reality of location filming literally came rushing down the track in 1895 when the Lumière Brothers shot a steam train coming into a station and the audience ran screaming out into the street. And the English countryside has acted as a backdrop to films for as long as cameras have been able to capture its likeness on celluloid. Even Thomas Hardy cooperated in the films based on his novels that appeared in the early years of the twentieth century. He sold the rights to *Far from the Madding Crowd* to a painter, Sir Hubert von Herkomer, for £150, with the option to make *The Mayor of Casterbridge* for an extra £25. Von Herkomer had illustrated some of the serialisation of *Tess of the d'Urbervilles* and intended to shoot his film in a studio he had erected in his garden, but died before the handle could be cranked on his camera.

Realising that films could be a good way to sell more of his books Hardy signed up *Far from the Madding Crowd* with the Turner Film Company in 1915. The studios were in Walton-on-Thames, some way from the story's Dorset origins, as was commented on by a critic writing in the *Bioscope* film magazine at the time. But the story and its real backgrounds came much closer together in 1921 when the Progress Film Company shot *The Mayor of Casterbridge* in authentic Dorset locations. Even in his eighties Hardy maintained an appreciative eye for actresses and very early one July morning he witnessed a scene being shot at Maiden Castle outside Dorchester, his eponymous Casterbridge. Hardy was amused to see that the local people took no notice of this strange intrusion, although he himself was somewhat surprised at the yellow make-up the cast wore. It was used to render their complexions a 'truer' shade of creamy white on the monochrome film stock, a technique also employed for television's *Z Cars* when all the Ford Zephyrs were similarly re-sprayed.

First Appearances

Being silent pictures with captions, the equipment that shot these early films was much smaller and lighter than the more sophisticated cameras that came later. J.J. Hissey's 1917 *The Road and the Inn* tells of the

motoring pioneer and author coming across a film crew in Surrey, shooting a film outside the White Hart in Witley. So small and unobtrusive were the crew, Hissey thought that the sight of two large mastiffs bounding through the door

of the tile-hung inn in order to chase a man out again, and the ensuing chase involving a mud-spattered motor car, was all too thrillingly real. A photograph he took of the scene shows a small wooden camera on a tripod behind which stand two chaps with their hands in their pockets. Men on the road, movie itinerants feeding the insatiable appetites of the new picture house audiences.

As the film industry developed it became more organised, the reversed-peak flat caps of handle-turning cameramen replaced by the green eye-shades of cigar-chomping directors. The big studios started to appear in an arc encircling London, from Elstree in the north to Shepperton in the southwest, with Pinewood and Denham as intermissions. The Ealing Studios were closer to London, but all were within a fast Lagonda run into the West End or a slow evening drive back home up into the beech ridges of the Chilterns. The cameras became leviathans, heavily padded (blimped) against unwanted noise, and moved slowly about on flat-surfaced sound stages. England could very easily be reduced to a cleverly-painted backdrop lit by giant Brute arc lamps; a controlled environment in which the English

top right
Quality hallmark for classic
English films

bottom right
Itinerant cameramen from
a *Punch* cartoon of 1923

weather, scourge of budget-conscious producers, could be reproduced at the throw of a switch. The great outdoors was very often the habitat only of second units sent out to get essential footage that could later be edited into the action.

But something else was happening away from the glitz and glamour of the studios. The documentary film was bringing a new, more edgy realism to cinema audiences waiting for the main feature, or perhaps more often to village halls and schools as a change from WI jam making and learning timetables. Foremost was the GPO Film Unit founded in 1933 under John Grierson, a successor to the Empire Marketing Board Film Unit. Here we saw the lives of coalminers, farmers, and factory workers, and, of course, the outright advertisements for the Post Office themselves. Most notable was *Night Mail* (1936) with its Britten score and Auden narrative echoing the piston beat of a steam train, not just delivering mail but sorting it as well in the Travelling Post Office. White exhaust smoke streaming out over the fields with 'This is the Night Mail crossing the border / Bringing the cheque and the postal order '.

Humphrey Jennings was one of the unit's film makers who went on to direct what were without doubt the finest officially sponsored films of the Second World War. Jennings's films went far beyond the propaganda value expected of them. Here was something truly enlightening, the very refreshing breath of air the medium needed. His 1942 *Listen to Britain* is a commentary-free evocation of twenty-four hours of life on the Home Front, freewheeling images edited with their natural sounds: the gracefully moving crowd on a Blackpool dance floor, a lunchtime concert attended by uniformed service men and women in a London church, camaraderie on a long train journey. We'd call it 'fly-on-the-wall' now, so used are we to the unblinking camera probing into every doubtful dark corner of our realities, but this isn't Jennings's style. His films are real, yes, but they also offer something else that we appear to have lost now, a true regard and a genuine affection and consideration for others.

1942 also saw the tiny village of Turville in its hidden Buckinghamshire valley making what I imagine was probably one of its first appearances on film. Alberto Cavalcanti brought his cameras out of the Ealing Studios to make *Went the Day*

Well, a disturbing view of the German military occupation of a quintessential English village: *Obersleutnants* in the church pulpit, *Wehmacht* in the post office. The *Sunday Times* said, 'At last, it seems, we are learning to make films with our own native material.'

Turville has seen everybody from Stanley Baxter and Leslie Philips in *Father Came Too* to Dawn French in *The Vicar of Dibley*. An alleyway between Turville cottages mysteriously appears as a Yorkshire village at the end of *Calendar Girls*, and this is the village that *Little Britain*'s Dafydd is the only gay in. As time moves on, a sense of real place seems to mean less and less. Budget restrictions and tax breaks result in a Dorset heroine turning up looking bewildered in the Channel Islands for *Under the Greenwood Tree* and the Isle of Man standing in for the Channel Islands in *Island at War*.

A Canterbury Tale

Medieval pilgrims jostle and joke their way across a bluff of the North Downs. A falconer releases a bird from his wrist and as it soars up into the sky it metamorphoses into a Spitfire descending over the pastures and hop fields of Kent. Six hundred years have past and the countryside is now hedged and ordered, but noisily filled with the sound of armoured vehicles and the shriek of an express train as it rapidly traverses a line dividing the fields. This is Powell and Pressburger's 1944 *A Canterbury Tale*, filmed as the long weary days of war could at last be seen to be coming to their conclusion.

The train pulls up in the dark at a blacked-out railway station, and after Charles Hawtrey shouts his head off we enter an England as lyrical and thought-provoking as anything filmed before or since. Local magistrate Culpepper longs to extol the virtues of England to newly-arrived American servicemen, the continuity of English life becoming his own personal mission. His obsessions affect all those around him, but ultimately they act as a catalyst for the redemption and fulfilment waiting for his fellow protagonists in Canterbury. Alfred Junge's designs for outsize bedrooms with fairy-tale four-posters and gloomy parlours with secret cupboards were realised at Denham, but once we go out through the doors and windows we are in the Kent countryside, the boyhood homeland of Michael Powell, and into scenes that distil a sense of Englishness as subtly as a quietly sung ballad. Women driving buses and women operating signal boxes, keeping it all going until their chaps arrive home. This is the England they're fighting for: the farms, the watermills, the wheelwrights and village pubs. Chilham and Canterbury are the principle locations, but some of the most idyllic and moving scenes are conducted up on the skylarked downs as the pale grass moves gently against deep summer skies.

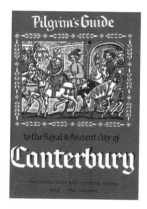

above
A post-war Canterbury guidebook

right
Canterbury Cathedral

Elgar

Another classic milestone in the filmed portrayals of the English landscape appeared on Sunday night television in 1962. On 11 November the BBC celebrated the one hundredth edition of its arts programme *Monitor* with Ken Russell's documentary *Elgar*. Here were fifty-six minutes of undiluted pleasure for anyone with even a passing interest in the composer, his music and the influences of the English countryside. It was unique at the time because Russell was able to use real actors, hitherto unknown in documentaries, but was sternly told by *Monitor*'s editor Huw Wheldon that they were not to be seen in close-up or allowed to speak. But what Russell did have was Elgar's music and the Malvern Hills. I don't think there can be anyone who has seen this film who can hear the *Introduction and Allegro for Strings* without

seeing Elgar on a pony, Elgar on a bike or Elgar flying a kite on the bare slopes of the hills. Purists said you should be able to listen to the music without the intrusion of the landscape dreams of an *enfant terrible* director, but they missed the point. This landscape *is* Elgar's music. Ken Russell remembers how Huw Wheldon saw the rough cut and complained that he wanted one of the sequences left on the cutting room floor. Russell blinked and said, 'But Huw, it's true, he *did* slide down the hills on a tea tray.'

Tom Jones

bottom

Two foyer cards for *Tom Jones* with Albert Finney as the eponymous hero and Susannah York, pictured here with Hugh Griffith as the irrepressible Squire Western

Within a few months of the *Monitor* birthday the English countryside again came startlingly to life as never before. After the successes of *A Taste of Honey* and *The Loneliness of the Long Distance Runner* director Tony Richardson took his cast and crew on what he promised would be '… a lovely ten weeks' holiday in the West Country'. Ten weeks shooting the rural scenes for John Osborne's adaptation of Henry Fielding's eighteenth-century novel, the quadruple Oscar-winning *Tom Jones* (1963). On its release I had to sneak into the Picture House in Leicester to see what was then an 'X' certificate film, but I don't suppose for one minute anybody took any notice. What I saw opened a door on to the English landscape that no book of photographs or even views from a train or motor coach window could possibly have done for me at the time. Cranborne Manor with its twin lodges seen in the first few frames, Cerne Abbas with its abbey gatehouse for locking up errant daughters. Langley Park for poaching, Cranborne Chase for hunting. Boating at Iwerne Stepleton, redcoats marching to the lusty singing of Rule Britannia at Hardy's Monument above Portesham. And Nettlecombe, deep in the Brendon Hills, doubling up for so much, including the parish church and, as a wet weather set, the Nettlecombe Court dog kennels cast as Newgate Prison. All meticulously captured by Walter Lassally's

The whole world loves **Tom Jones!**

X

ALBERT FINNEY   SUSANNAH YORK
HUGH GRIFFITH   EDITH EVANS
JOAN GREENWOOD · "*Tom Jones*"
DIANE CILENTO

GEORGE and the guest appearance of
DEVINE   DAVID TOMLINSON   JOHN OSBORNE   TONY RICHARDSON   EASTMAN COLOUR   A WOODFALL PRODUCTION

above
Film poster for Tony
Richardson's *Tom Jones*
(1963)

right
Chastleton House,
Gloucestershire, Sir
Thomas Booby's house in
Joseph Andrews (1977)

camera with lenses filtered by a veil from a
1920s' lady's silk hat. Here eighteenth-century
life became utterly convincing, Georgian
England making an extraordinary transition
from Hogarthian paintings and prints to full-
blooded realism.

Richardson tried to repeat the massive
success the film enjoyed with *Joseph Andrews*
(1977) at Chastleton House and Bath but the
original youthful exuberance was lost. David
Watkin's photography is, however, simply
astounding, particularly in the ballroom
sequence and in a flashback involving actor
Ronald Pickup.

Far from the Madding Crowd

For sixteen weeks John Schlesinger extended the frame into Panavision for *Far from the Madding Crowd* (1967). Thomas Hardy's classic tale of one woman and her three lovers plays out against the magnificent all-embracing landscapes and nineteenth-century agricultural practices of Dorset. Nic Roeg's camera sweeps bleak downland above a brooding English Channel, and captures sheep pastures and cornfields enfolded in tree-topped hills and bathing machines facing

the sea on a wave-pounded Weymouth beach. Maiden Castle was once again pressed into service, this time as the location for a display of swordsmanship in the hands of a red-coated ego. And the buildings: Waddon Manor above Portesham for doom-laden William Boldwood and his Dalmatians, Bloxworth Manor near Bere Regis for wilful Bathsheba Everdene, Horton Tower north of Wimborne for Sergeant Troy and his ill-advised cockfighting bet. Steady Gabriel Oak's domesticity is really only glimpsed in his precariously-positioned mobile shepherd's hut.

Her romance with three men becomes a bold adventure

ANGLO AMALGAMATED FILM DISTRIBUTORS present a JOSEPH JANNI production

JULIE CHRISTIE

TERENCE STAMP
PETER FINCH
ALAN BATES

"FAR FROM THE MADDING CROWD"

with FIONA WALKER introducing PRUNELLA RANSOME
PANAVISION® TECHNICOLOR®
Screenplay by FREDERIC RAPHAEL Directed by JOHN SCHLESINGER

above

Michael Reeves's
Witchfinder General (1968)

As Schlesinger's viewfinder scanned sunny upland slopes, others were toiling in darker realms. Cinema audiences watching horror films at this time were usually distanced from their subject matter by the artificialities of glossy set-bound Hammer Films. Almost always set in eastern European countries, their backgrounds were carefully constructed in Bray Studios near Maidenhead and if a chase sequence were needed, they just humped the camera out to a country house driveway, usually lined with rhodedendrons. Invariably they featured a *gasthof* where an innkeeper wiping down a silver-lidded steiner would warn, 'Oh no, Sir, nobody goes up there, Sir, especially at night'.

Witchfinder General

Barely into his twenties, director Michael Reeves was determined to change all that. He took his audience roughly by the hand, marched them out of the cinema and deposited them in seventeenth-century East Anglia, stood them up against wind-blown oaks and said, 'Right. Just watch this.' From the opening scene in *Witchfinder General* (1968) of a woman being dragged screaming to a hilltop gallows through to a particularly graphic dismembering in Orford Castle, Reeves just didn't let go.

A sense of place was vital to how he told the story of Matthew Hopkins, a Manningtree lawyer who took it upon himself during the Civil War to roam the countryside with his assistant Sterne torturing confessions of witchcraft from innocent single ladies who owned black cats. Reeves and his writer Tom Baker didn't want to just hand a script over to a location finder and so for weeks they scoured the Suffolk and Norfolk countryside like a latterday Hopkins and Sterne, whittling out places with particular resonance for their film version of what is actually a true story. The Ministry of Works nervously let them in to Orford Castle;

Lavenham marketplace warmed to the burning of a 'witch'. Near Thetford, the juxtaposition of Rushford College (albeit with Teulon's 1855 porch) and St John's church opposite became the pivotal Brandeston. This was the village where in chilling reality the name of John Lowes, one the witchfinder's more notable victims, can be seen in the list of clergy up on the south wall of All Saints church. But it's the sparsely-populated East Anglian countryside, particularly around Grimes Graves, that most characterises Reeves's vision. Wide, unenclosed sheep pastures ringed by oaks, dense forest rides with bracken closing in on all sides and loose chalk lanes between silver birches where Master Hopkins could hold his tall witchfinder's hat against the wind as he slowly rode to his next appointment.

top
Rushford College, Norfolk

bottom right
The Guild Hall, Lavenham, scene of the infamous ladder burning in *Witchfinder General*

bottom left
Orford Castle, Suffolk

The Go-Between

A more comfortable East Anglia is evoked in L.P. Hartley's 1953 novel of innocence and illicit passion that tells the story of a schoolboy's 1900 summer holiday at his classmate's Norfolk country home. In *The Go-Between* Hartley wrote, 'To my mind's eye, my buried memories of Brandham Hall are like effects of chiaroscuro, patches of light and dark: it is only with effort that I can see them in terms of colour.'

With Harold Pinter's screenplay in hand Joseph Losey brought the colour to Hartley's fiction in 1970, re-creating Brandham at Melton Constable Hall, a red-brick Stuart mansion in empty parkland near the old railway junction village of Melton Constable in Norfolk. Steeped in a summer heatwave the house and its occupants are seen through the eyes of Leo Colston as he accustomises himself to a world apart from his gentle home life with his recently-widowed mother. Licking a spoon in kitchens discovered down internally-glazed corridors, listening in his attic bedroom to a song being sung in a distant drawing room. Watching bathers in an almost sea-like Norfolk Broad (Hickling) and basking in glory at having saved the day in the cricket match (shot on the

green at Thornage). Running across the park and through hot fields to the brick and flint house and outbuildings of tenant farmer Ted Burgess, hurrying back with the covert letter for Marian at the Hall. And always the sense that something is going on out of sight, the social machineries of a large country house playing out their relentless rituals.

One evocative image breaks down the barrier that often stands between reality and fiction. After Leo and Marian's return from a shopping trip to Norwich, with a scene set in its curiously-named Tombland, there is a static shot of the park standing in stifling heat. A train whistle breaks the stillness and a herd of deer raise up their heads in watchful alertness. For a brief moment, fictitious Brandham perhaps becomes Melton Constable Hall of 1900 with the railway junction just over the trees.

above
Promotional booklet for *The Go-Between* (1970)

top right
Essential film director kit: the viewfinder for ranging shots, to be worn around the neck at all times on location

opposite
Melton Constable Hall (*built* 1664–70), Norfolk, one of the finest Grade 1 listed buildings in the country

GUIDEBOOK ENGLAND

As roads in England started to progress beyond muddy impassable tracks into the first semblances of proper roads, the guide and map publishers moved in. John Ogilby brought out his *Britannia* in 1675: *A Geographical and Historical description of the Principal Roads thereof consisting of One Hundred Maps of Main Roads.* Ogilby further promoted his achievement by boldly stating that 25,000 miles of road had been covered. In fact it was 7,500, still remarkable for its time. The strip maps not only had a compass rose against each section, they also described the country on either side of a particular road. Later, in 1771, Daniel Paterson – 'Assistant to the Quarter Master General of His Majesty's Forces' – produced his *New and Accurate description of all the Direct and Principal Cross Roads in Great Britain*, a guide that continued with revisions until 1832.

J.J. Hissey

Paterson's AA handbook of the coaching era was still being used by John James Hissey when he embarked on his travels around England, which lasted from the 1880s up to the First World War. Hissey's travels were made in everything from phaetons to pioneering Daimler motor cars, and resulted in beautifully produced books with titles like *Across England in a Dog Cart* (1891), all illustrated with either his lichen-encrusted drawings or photographs. He tended to get a bit overwrought when confronted by the beauty of the English landscape, particularly after a storm, but his descriptions of village and roadside inns are rare insights into what a Victorian or Edwardian traveller could have expected. Hissey rarely travelled on his own, and even when you think for two-thirds of a book he is alone (or, with only a chum or his wife) you can suddenly be introduced to a groom or a mechanic who hitherto had been invisible. Hissey was also bemoaning the loss of his England; he hated the intrusion of the railways and couldn't understand the appeal of plate glass shop windows.

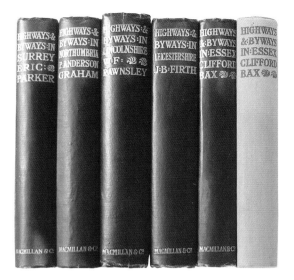

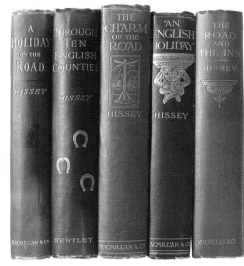

Highways & Byways

Macmillan's Highways & Byways series continued the impression of well-heeled gentlemen exploring the countryside during the day and relaxing in coaching inns in the evening: '… we make the best of five miles through the failing light home to the "George" '. Full of anecdotes and curious histories they were sumptuously illustrated by leading contemporary artists. The spidery line of Joseph Pennell, the storybook style of Hugh Thomson. The prestigious series was founded in 1900 for Macmillan by Frederick Griggs, out in all weathers on his motorcycle with his sharpened pencils for, amongst others, *Highways & Byways in Lincolnshire* (1914), *Leicestershire* (1926) and the last volume *Essex* (1939), which he was illustrating when he died. It was very successfully worked on and completed by S.R. Badmin (q.v.), whose assured pen brought a character and human scale not hitherto experienced in these dark blue volumes with their fat gold titles. *Essex* can be found in both this livery and in very plain pale blue boards, wartime bombing having interrupted the binding process.

Edward Thomas

The Highways & Byways' style perhaps fits Edward Thomas's description of 'the Norfolk-jacket school of writing'. He knocked it all into a cocked-hat with his books, like *In Pursuit of Spring* (1914), a weather-sodden account of a cycle tour made with his alter ego the 'Other Man' from London to the Quantocks in 1913. Thomas disliked having to write travel books for a living, but just after the publication of this volume he was in the Artists Rifles and, encouraged to do so by Robert Frost, began writing poetry for the first time. He was barely three years away from his untimely death at Arras and premature legacy of some of the finest poems in the English language. They are instilled with a sense of place, of making us see with his eyes as, say, he sits in pubs simply taking it all in while drinking his beer. His very first poem 'Up in the Wind' has the quiet observer sitting in a remote pub up amongst Hampshire beeches listening to a girl complaining as she worked: 'A public-house! It may be public for birds, / Squirrels and suchlike, ghosts of charcoal-burners / And highwaymen…'

One of the last poems (written in 1916 and later called 'The Watchers') finds Thomas looking out from another pub window. As with all the best writers, it is what's left unsaid that lingers. I always imagine that this is a dull summer afternoon with perhaps a distant rumble of thunder and the sound of a clock in another room:

> *By the ford at the town's edge*
> *Horse and carter rest:*
> *the carter smokes on the bridge*
> *Watching the water press in swathes about his*
> *   horse's chest.*

> *From the inn one watches, too,*
> *In the room for visitors*
> *That has no fire, but a view*
> *And many cases of stuffed fish, vermin, and*
> *   kingfishers.*

I have perhaps strayed from guidebooks *per se*, but I think it's worth noting that when Thomas was asked why he enlisted in the army while there was much he felt at odds with in England he answered by picking up a handful of soil and said, 'Literally, for this'.

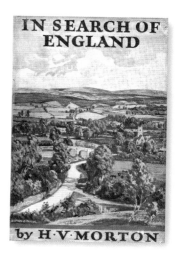 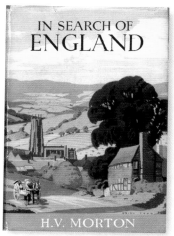 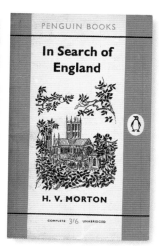

H.V. Morton

The dusty roads of England that had gradually declined in use since the end of the coaching era and the arrival of the railways suddenly had their peace shattered by the first backfirings of the motor car. By the 1920s this handbuilt luxury for the very rich was now mass-produced and available at a much more modest cost. The motoring public had arrived; the Sunbeams, Austins, Talbot Coupés taking to the roads with picnic hampers and the new touring maps. Back home they relaxed in front of the fire with an H.V. Morton or an S.P.B. Mais book to find out where they'd been and where to go next.

Henry Canova Vollam Morton's first book was *The Heart of London* (1925), a compilation of his popular newspaper columns, but he was soon worrying his boss at the *Daily Express* to let him have a Bullnose Morris to drive all over England. The idea came to him as he lay ill with meningitis in Palestine and the resulting book

In Search of England (1927), published by Methuen, ran to countless impressions. My copy is the eighteenth edition, printed only six years later. Morton had matinée idol looks with moustache and trilby, his relaxed style immensely readable and perfectly suited to his roving eye and ear for dialogue. Here he is after seeing Christchurch Priory in Dorset:

I was walking on with a soul full of Norman transepts when a maiden stood before me and looked. She had the greyest eyes. 'Would you,' she said, 'like a lobster?'

In *The English* (1998) Jeremy Paxman writes of Morton's thoughts during his illness:

It never seems to have struck him as odd that when he thought of the England he imagined he would never see again he didn't conjure up St Paul's Cathedral or the townscapes of his youth, but villages, church bells, thatched cottages and woodsmoke rising in the clear air.

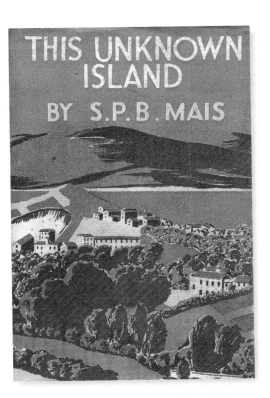

S.P.B. Mais

Stuart Petre Brodie Mais was once as familiar to wireless listeners as John Humphrys is today. In the early 1930s everyone tuned in on a Monday night to hear his programme *This Unknown Island*, a series of talks about England for which Mais dashed about all over the country by car and train and then dashed back again to sit in front of a big BBC microphone. In 1933 he broadcast *A Letter From America*, years before Alistair Cooke had the idea, and later a wartime cookery programme called *Kitchen Front*. One of the most prolific travel writers of the twentieth century (around 200 books including rambling guides for the

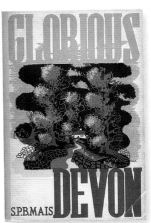

Southern Railway (q.v.) and Great Western Railway holiday guides) he was an eccentric, warm-hearted man who played village cricket (badly by all accounts) and rightly earned himself the title of 'Ambassador of the Countryside'. His style was bright and brisk, a 'gentle sergeant major' who always said exactly what was on his mind. In *Oh! To be in England* he insists that the only way to travel to Brighton is by First Class Pullman and, 'Having arrived at your hotel, you will order the fire to be lit in your bedroom at six o'clock, so that you can dress for dinner in comfort…' Quite so, but I think his tongue was very firmly in his cheek.

PREHISTORIC ENGLAND

GRAHAME CLARK

ENGLISH VILLAGES AND HAMLETS

HUMPHREY PAKINGTON

THE ENGLISH COTTAGE

PARISH CHURCHES OF ENGLAND

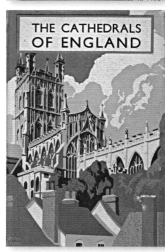

THE CATHEDRALS OF ENGLAND

THE OLD TOWNS OF ENGLAND

CLIVE ROUSE

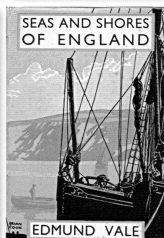

SEAS AND SHORES OF ENGLAND

EDMUND VALE

THE ENGLISH GARDEN

RALPH DUTTON

THE ENGLISH ABBEY

F. H. CROSSLEY

THE COUNTRYMAN'S ENGLAND

DOROTHY HARTLEY

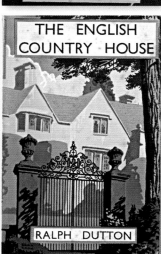

THE ENGLISH COUNTRY HOUSE

RALPH DUTTON

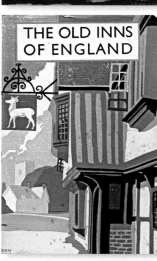

THE OLD INNS OF ENGLAND

Batsford and Brian Cook

Both Morton's and Mais's books sported colourful jackets that cashed in on the vogue for depicting a stylised England in flat colours like the new railway posters. Mais's compilation of his *This Unknown Island* talks (1932) has a front cover so bright it looks more like the Italian Lakes, but this is nothing compared to what hit the bookshops in the same year. Most books still had a dust jacket for that purpose alone, keeping the product clean. (They were never meant to stay with the book after purchase, a fact that stayed with readers right up to our times. Having religiously collected a set of H.V. Mortons in their rare jackets for my father's Christmas present I was stunned to discover he'd thrown the covers away.) But the appearance of publisher Batsford's books were transformed when illustrator and family member Brian Cook (he later changed his name to Batsford in order to keep the name alive) discovered the Jean Berté printing process and utilised it to produce covers for the English Life series. The high intensity inks used were water-based and needed special rubber rollers, but with the overlaying of three primary colours, grey and a defining black the effect was stunning, if a little unpredictable. Cook eventually tired of the amount of work involved for the printers in cutting stencils from his flat-colour originals and reverted to more traditional methods for later series, but the extremely collectable English Life books have earnt a unique place in both design and publishing history.

Batsford published an impressive list of titles majoring on topography and architecture, and even had a small role in the early pre-war days of our next guidebook subject, perhaps the very best of them all.

Shell Guides

In 1934 John Betjeman left the *Architectural Review* magazine and was brought into Shell by Jack Beddington to instigate a new series of county guidebooks. 'Beddioleman', as Betjeman typically called him, was, along with Frank Pick of the London Underground, one of the most publicity-conscious managers of the age. He was the man who turned Shell lorry sides into moving art galleries with posters by some of the most talented artists and designers working in pre-war Britain. Graham Sutherland, Paul Nash, Edward Ardizzone and Rex Whistler all saw their work sell petrol and oils to an ever-expanding motoring public. Even Lord Berners painted his folly tower in its clump of firs above Faringdon and designed the cover for the 1935 *Wiltshire*. Beddington was quick to realise that the promotion of Shell's

EVERYWHERE YOU GO

THE GREAT GLOBE SWANAGE   BY GRAHAM SUTHERLAND

YOU CAN BE SURE OF SHELL

products through the Guides would be a way for the company to introduce motoring as a means, not an end in itself.

Beddington advanced £20 for a mock-up to be produced and Betjeman insisted on, and won, the right to take total responsibility for everything, from who should write them to the typography and what colour paper they should be printed on. He wrote:

The Guides came into existence chiefly because there seemed no half-way house in modern typographical literature between the fulsome paean of a town clerk's brochure and the exhaustive and sometimes exhausting antiquarian accounts published either in local pamphlets or in Methuen's Little Guides...

ORDSHIRE A Shell Guide by J

UTLAND III A Shell Guide by W.G

folk Wilhelmine Harrod & C.L.
A SHELL GUIDE

rset A Shell Guide·Micha

OPSHIRE A Shell Guide | John Piper &

FOLK A Shell Guide by N

colnshire Jack Yates & Hen
A SHELL GUIDE

efordshire A Shell Guide by Davi

byshire Henry Thorold
A SHELL GUIDE

cestershire A Shell Guide by Anthor

evon A Shell Guide by Bria

LANTEGLOS - BY - FOWEY
but
MOTORISTS BUY SHELL

top
Advertisement from
Cornwall, illustrated by
Edward Bawden

bottom
The first Shell Guide,
Cornwall, published by the
Architectural Press (1934)

Cornwall was published in June 1934. It was just about as idiosyncratic as a Shell Guide was ever to get; not bad for the first one. Edited by Betjeman himself (this county was after all his family's second home), it is a wonderfully undisciplined scrapbook of styles and content. Behind a cover depicting a pipe-smoking fisherman, Mrs Tremaine's farmhouse recipes

jostle for attention with local hunt details and tide tables. One turns the page from fishing notes written by the editor's father to be confronted by a double-page spread filled with a dramatic uncaptioned photograph of a sailing ship foundering on rocks. The typography is as eclectic as a Victorian typefounder's catalogue: thin-serifed Bodonis comfortable with Old English black letter. Pink paper is slipped in with content as varied as the photograph of a blind Primitive Methodist, to tips on picnicing that include the exhortation 'Don't forget to wrap sandwiches in greaseproof paper', all printed in deep blue ink. Shell's only walk-on part seems to be an ad. at the back, but even that is a gentle Edward Bawden illustrated pun. The whole thing is kept together with a spiral wire binding.

It set the tone for the pre-war editions; mates and contemporaries of Betjeman queuing up to write Guides. Paul Nash for the first edition of *Dorset*, with his own photographs and water-colours, his brother John for *Buckinghamshire*, and, marking the start of the famous Shell Guide double act, John Piper taking on *Oxfordshire* in 1938. Betjeman met him in 1937, and there couldn't have been a better pairing.

below

Covers for the Penguin Buildings of England series

Piper the painter, designer and photographer with a uniquely accurate understanding of the unsung and neglected, and Betjeman the poet, writer and broadcaster who shared Piper's childhood passion for racing around country lanes on a bike looking at churches. Theirs became a mission to include in the books everything hitherto left out by stuffy guides now

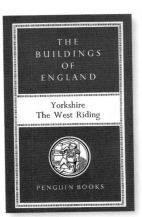 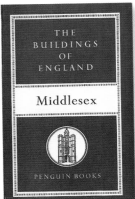 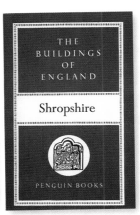

floundering in the new age of the motor car. They wrote, photographed and laughed their way around Shropshire as the storm clouds gathered over Europe, the war bringing a temporary shelving of the Guide until sunnier times saw its republication in 1951.

The post-war Guides brought a less temporary feel to the books. Now they had proper bindings and the typography was whipped into line. The pre-war editions were reprinted, still with delightfully odd additions peppering the text: Brian Watson's *Devon* giving advice on how to charm adders and Thomas Sharp's revised *Northumberland* with Bewick engravings as tailpieces. Of course they weren't confined to England. The rest of Britain had their Shell Guides, not least *The West Coast of Scotland* where Stephen Bone goes on about Highland fairies being pretty well exclusively women. But Piper and Betjeman stuck to where they were most at ease, deep in the English counties. *Shropshire* appeared in 1951, the same year that Penguin published the first volume in the Buildings of England series, *Middlesex*. These monumental books were written by a German émigré, Niklaus Pevsner, who Betjeman had dubbed 'Herr Dokter' in his exasperation at what he saw as the clinical cataloguing of buildings.

DORSET
Compiled by
PAUL NASH

SHELL GUIDE
Three and Sixpence

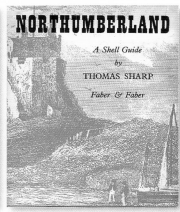

NORTHUMBERLAND

A Shell Guide
by
THOMAS SHARP

Faber & Faber

Worcestershire
by J. LEES-MILNE
A Shell Guide

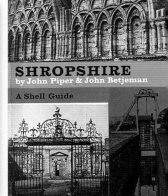

SHROPSHIRE
by John Piper & John Betjeman

A Shell Guide

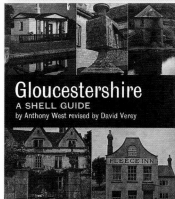

Gloucestershire
A SHELL GUIDE
by Anthony West revised by David Verey

FLEECE INN

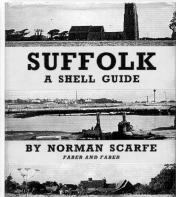

SUFFOLK
A SHELL GUIDE

BY NORMAN SCARFE
FABER AND FABER

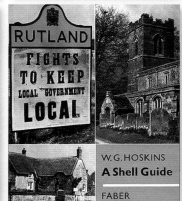

RUTLAND
FIGHTS
TO KEEP
LOCAL GOVERNMENT
LOCAL

W. G. HOSKINS
A Shell Guide

FABER

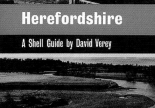

Herefordshire

A Shell Guide by David Verey

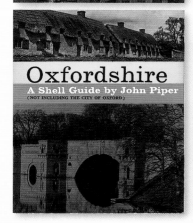

Oxfordshire
A SHELL GUIDE by John Piper
(NOT INCLUDING THE CITY OF OXFORD)

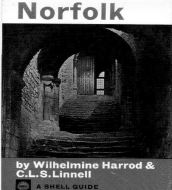

Norfolk

by Wilhelmine Harrod &
C.L.S. Linnell
A SHELL GUIDE

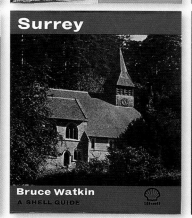

Surrey

Bruce Watkin
A SHELL GUIDE   Shell

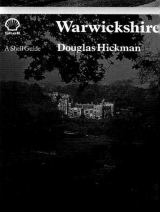

Shell
A Shell Guide

Warwickshire
Douglas Hickman

KENT

SHELL GUIDES
Two and Sixpence

HAMPSHIRE

BY JOHN RAYNER

Shell Guide 2'6

Wiltshire

A SHELL GUIDE by David Verey

Cornwall

John Betjeman A Shell Guide

THE ISLE OF WIGHT

A Shell Guide by Pennethorne Hughes

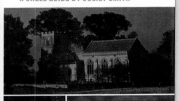

Northamptonshire

& the Soke of Peterborough

A SHELL GUIDE BY JULIET SMITH

Dorset

A SHELL GUIDE
by Michael Pitt-Rivers

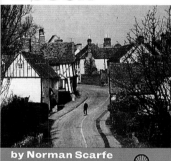

Essex

by Norman Scarfe

A SHELL GUIDE

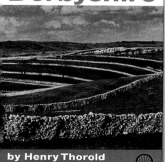

Derbyshire

by Henry Thorold
A SHELL GUIDE

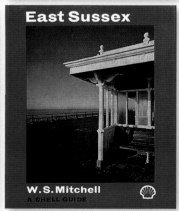

East Sussex

W. S. Mitchell
A SHELL GUIDE

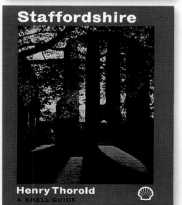

Staffordshire

Henry Thorold
A SHELL GUIDE

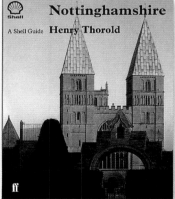

Shell
A Shell Guide

Nottinghamshire
Henry Thorold

ff

A selection of Shell County Guides
from Paul Nash's *Dorset* (1935)
to Henry Thorold's
Nottinghamshire (1984)

Seven years later Pevsner was also in Shropshire, assistants scribbling away in the back of an Austin driven by his wife as he barked out architectural features. The entry for Bucknell epitomises the difference between the Betjeman / Piper approach and the Pevsner inventories. The latter only mentions the church in terse detail; the Shell Guide quickly mentions that it's basically Victorian but then goes on to talk with relish about the railway station, '… L.M.S. [London Midland Scottish], dated 1860, … a neat Gothic building with bargeboards, Tudor-style chimneys and free-stone walls'.

The Shell Guides' photography started to be credited, and as the control over images became increasingly the preserve of John Piper, in 1962 he became joint editor with Betjeman. W.G. Hoskins's 1963 *Rutland* became, along with the hardback *Nottinghamshire*, one of the rarest Guides to collect; my first copy was bought in a musty schoolroom in Uppingham, a thin book that was either flood damaged or suffering from total immersion in a reader's bath, the pages curving into those distinctive series of arcs made by dried-out waterlogged paper.

opposite
Bucknell station in
Shropshire, photographed
in 1978

above
Edwin Smith's
photograph of Hidcote,
Gloucestershire (1970)

Faber and Faber, the Guides' publishers, were giving a more cohesive style to the books, the covers using photographs with coloured tints and interesting sans serif fonts. John Piper was providing more and more pictures himself, taken on his new Hasselblad and developed in a darkroom installed in the stables at Stonor near his home. He could often be found crouching in dimly lit churches, lighting medieval fonts with a single portable oil lamp, having dampened the decoration with a wet sponge to bring out the detail. Another name increasingly appearing in the photography credit list was Edwin Smith. John Betjeman wrote in the *Daily Telegraph*:

Mr Smith is a genius at photography. Though in monochrome his photographs are as full of the suggestion of colour as are those marvellous etchings of Norfolk which Cotman made at the beginning of the last century…makes one proud to live in England.

John Betjeman resigned from the Guides in 1967, after a major row developed with Shell over their unwillingness to endorse a comment by Juliet Smith in her *Northamptonshire*. It left him pondering whether, '… it had been worth it, having all those jokes with typography.' As the series moved into the seventies everything became more formalised: no listings of 'early closing days' now, but still sparkling with the unfashionable views of the writers and photography lovingly printed in a darkroom. The thrusting eighties saw them running out of steam. Monochrome pictures, and old buffers getting overworked by bellcotes and lancet windows must have seemed oddly out-of-step with a money-obsessed age. Colour photographs on the jackets couldn't halt their decline, and I suppose Shell had more on their corporate minds than gently showing off English counties. So they never got round to doing Yorkshire, Lancashire, Cheshire, Bedfordshire. Not even a half-hearted paperback resurrection of the series at the end of the decade using colour pictures throughout could revive their fortunes.

 But sometimes when I sit in a church porch in the rain with a Shell Guide telling me not to miss the box pews, I think of Betjeman and Piper in some kind of parallel universe, still out there completing the series. Piper on his knees sponging down the font, Betjeman in his boater throwing his head back in laughter.

Shell and The Shilling Guides

below

A book made from the Shell Nature Study posters: *Fossils, Insects and Reptiles*, painted by Tristram Hillier and *The Shell Book of Roads*, painted by David Gentleman

Shell's promotional programmes in the 1950s were outstanding. Posters were sent to schools on a variety of natural history and topographical subjects, sturdily printed and held by metal strips top and bottom with a hook ready for hanging. We had them all round my junior school hall, a visual feast of birds' eggs, wild flowers, fossils and reptiles. The counties were well represented and there was a series of posters by David Gentleman on roads. Each nature study and county poster contained a beautiful painting comprising any number of salient items in one scene, all annotated with a single colour numbered key. If ever I come across the smell of stale milk I think of them, the school hall parquet floor was permanently impregnated by the spillages of milk monitors, of whom I was one. (The most important official position I've ever occupied.)

The natural history and roads subjects got adapted into press advertisements and books, and the county paintings appeared as the covers for The Shilling Guides series in 1963, a joint piece of marketing with BP. If one can't lay hands on the original posters, these little yellow books are the next best thing because the illustration is reproduced in its entirety, using up most of the front and back covers. Each one is a perfect evocation of an individual county, once again a superb example of generous resources spent on employing the cream of contemporary commercial artists. The Shilling Guides were eventually published as a single fat volume, *The Shell and BP Guide to Britain*, and the paintings were once again pressed into service, but sadly they suffer from being tightly cropped to fit the proportion of a single page.

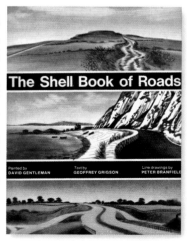

THE SHILLING GUIDES

DORSET

THE SHILLING GUIDES

DORSET

THE SHILLING GUIDES

SHROPSHIRE

THE SHILLING GUIDES

KENT

THE SHILLING GUIDES

LEICESTERSHIRE AND RUTLAND

THE SHILLING GUIDES

SUFFOLK

THE SHILLING GUIDES

HAMPSHIRE
and the Isle of Wight

...e Shilling Guides ...d paintings originally ...ecuted for the Shell ...unty Guides posters. ...e artists in this selection

are: *Dorset*, John Nash; *Shropshire*, S.R. Badmin; *Kent*, Rowland Hilder; *Leicestershire & Rutland* (back cover shown), Barry

Driscoll; *Suffolk*, John O'Connor; *Hampshire & The Isle of Wight*, Keith Shackleton

National Benzole

National Benzole's branding came through very strongly in their early 1960s' paperback books, although they had dispensed of the slightly whiffy Benzole for their new trademark with its stylised Mercury in his winged hat. The series majored on individual buildings, illustrated using lithography by Paul Sharp (quick and sketchy drawings, very much of their time) and, as it quaintly says in small type at the back, 'writing by E.M. Hatt'. Editor Sir Hugh Casson made sure he got his name in glorious isolation on the front covers. These are highly underrated little books, packed with useful information and county-by-county gazetteers.

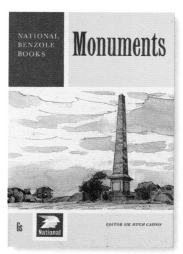

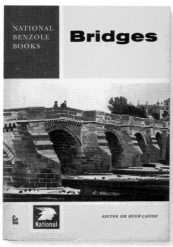

bottom left
Vision of England books,
with covers by Kenneth
Rowntree

bottom right
Illustration by the same
artist for *The Isle of Wight*

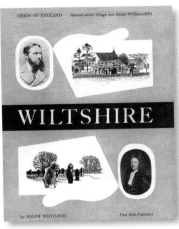

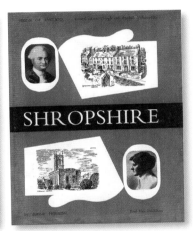

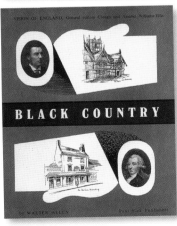

Vision of England

The Vision of England books were introduced in the late 1940s as 'a new series of personal books on the English Scene'. Published by Paul Elek, they came under the editorship of Clough and Amabel Williams-Ellis, presumably when Clough took time off from creating the opera scenery village of Portmeirion. They were, if anything, slightly odder than the Shell Guides, using photographs grouped together and illustrations interspersed throughout the text. Authors included Olive Cook (wife of Edwin Smith), Geoffrey Grigson and Ralph Whitlock. Amongst the artists were Kenneth Rowntree, Barbara Jones and Michael Rothenstein.

A PARTICULAR KIND OF PUB

During my past wanderings, a-foot and a-wheel, many a pleasant evening have I spent in the ancient parlours of such inns to which kindly Fate led me…

The Road and the Inn, J.J. Hissey

opposite
Aged innkeepers and pub regulars were always favourite images for breweries. Detail of an Everards beer mat from the 1930s

Fate has certainly led me into a few pubs too. Village ale houses, town boozers, roadhouse stop-offs, city taverns, crossroad inns, corner locals– all have at some time pulled me in and sat me down with a pint. We love our pubs in England, we support them with fierce loyalties, castigate them when they dare to re-paint the nicotine-stained ceilings and go into decline when the Bass is taken off and replaced by something called Arse's Bottom.

But what is the unmitigated English pub like? Is it a 'gastro' with salmon fishcakes, over-priced Chablis and an unwelcoming stare for the grizzled local who used to sit at the end of the bar? Hardly. Is it a town centre tavern condemned by corporate greed to be a cattle pen of drunken louts of both sexes throwing up 'alcopops' in the gutter outside? Er, no. In fact the pubs I like best are now getting to be treasured rarities and by the time you read this many will have changed beyond all recognition or quite simply disappeared. Rest assured the Tobacco Police will soon call time on any hangers-on anyway.

So maybe we should draw up some guidelines as to what constitutes this mythic pub, within the terms of this book's prejudices at least. One night myself and a few pals drew up a kind of *desiderata* of expectations. I think it got left on the pub table, but here's the gist of it.

The quality of the beer is a given and, without getting all tweed-jacket-with-elbow-patches over it, that means cask-conditioned ale that's actually watched over by a master brewer rather than by a security guard staring blankly at a computer screen. The beer should be dispensed by pulling a wooden or ceramic pump handle rather than by flicking a switch on a grotesque plastic dispenser that looks like a cobra's head. Even better if the beer is drawn straight from a racked-up barrel on a low brick shelf. Sometimes a pub will meet every other criteria but only have one nozzle spurting out carbonated disinfectant; in this case we should go for a decent bottled beer or hit the single malts.

You'll be lucky to see a sign hanging outside (it'll be upside down in the hedge) and there'll

be possibly no lighting except a bulb winking through the curtains. I tried to get outside toilets put on the list, accessible only by a walk across a dark yard, but a few raised eyebrows meant it got relegated to a kind of appendix that also included roller towels instead of hand dryers. The girls baulked at this and a compromise was reached whereby the dryers were in only if there weren't rubber chewing gum traps in the urinals. Different tables and chairs was a good one, rather than identikit high-gloss furniture, perhaps even a sofa with horsehair spilling out of it. No music, not even a folk group on Thursday nights (although I insisted that ones that didn't put fingers in their ears might be allowed) and certainly no gaming machines. Genuine advertising material like 1959 Babycham showcards on the mantelpiece are okay if they've been there since 1959. Serving food was a worry, but we thought something in a bowl with just a fork might be alright.

There was a heated debate about bar staff, with a preference amongst the blokes for someone like an Ovaltine Dairy Maid (the one on page 17 would do) but in fact some of the best pubs we know are run either by elderly couples or by widows who sit knitting by a coke

fire in the bar waiting for customers to come in. Town pubs should have open fires in a range of small rooms maintained by white-haired retainers in long green aprons hobbling about with coal buckets. Children would be welcome provided they kept to a wired-off compound at the bottom of the garden.

Whilst struggling to remember this check list I asked one of the other committee members if he could help. I should have known better. Leigh Hooper is an Englishman who sits on an Italian mountain side reading the *Spectator* and he forwarded me a long list, almost all of which was unprintable. But there were some very wry observations. Hooper says if there's a sign saying 'Coaches Welcome' drive on, similarly if there's a 12ft tall plastic camel / elephant / Mickey Mouse in the garden. If the specials blackboard has more than six starters and ten main courses demand to take a look in the deepfreeze. Sparkling clean glasses should be a reasonable indicator of care and efficiency, but Hooper admits this is a bit difficult to ascertain without going round the back of the bar when you first walk in. (I'm not sure about this one. I once saw the ninety-year-old bar maid in a favourite pub breathe on a spirit glass and then wipe it on a corner of her blouse.) He also went on about leaving a pub immediately if you saw a copy of *Truck* magazine on a table, but I think this may be getting off the point.

The reality is, as always, a hotchpotch of some of these things and other point scorers we never thought of, like a pub recently that suddenly became very appealing because a) it had a draught beer called Signalman's Stout and b) a television to watch the Grand National on. When normally televisions are obviously excluded at all costs.

The Rugglestone Inn, Widecombe

A pub I drank in when living on South Dartmoor in the 1970s probably comes as near as any to ticking off every item on the pub wish-list. There are two pubs in Widecombe, the one everyone knows up on the main street, and one that my new landlady told me 'Might suit you better'. Reached down a lane by the church that winds down to Venton, The Rugglestone Inn sits on a bend; low, granite-walled and with a tiny stream running right in front of the front door.

But before I go any further I have to tell you it has changed. Not immeasurably, and on my last visit (a few years ago admittedly) there was still much I recognised and I was warmly welcomed by the 'new' people who very obviously appreciated what had gone before. All too often pubs suffer from having their heart ripped out without any thought of retaining certain elements that ensure some kind of continuity. However, I spent an inordinate amount of time here, an 'early doors' session after returning from work in Newton Abbot, and a 'late doors' after supper. (My daughter thinks that 'early doors' means just getting to the pub earlier.) I'm amazed I can remember anything about it at all, but here is a brief account of what has stayed with me: the pub, the drinking, and that most vital ingredient of all– the people.

I'm pretty sure there was no overt signing, maybe just a simple wooden plank in maroon paint. It looked more cottage than pub, and after the latch was lifted on the door a corridor led down to a pantry on the left with a half-door that had a narrow shelf attached to the top of the lower half. Plymouth Bass was taken from racked-up barrels, glasses from a set of shelves above a worktop where stood odd bottles of Worthington E and a tin tray advertising Pony. The till was a wooden box, the accounting and stock control a paper pad and a Biro. Opposite was the room where we drank. No 'saloon' or 'lounge' here. Against one wall was a long bench at a table covered with a brown oilcloth, to the left a huge oak settle and a little table with a long case clock furiously ticking above it. The mantlepiece had a showcard for Bass with a pretty girl on it; a round table sat next to a cream-painted window seat.

All floor surfaces were a kind of concrete skim. The toilet was outside, just a little distance down the garden path at the side of the stream, lit by a bare bulb and complete with a chain pull. Everything was spotlessly clean.

above left

A 1975 photograph of The Rugglestone Inn, Widecombe-in-the-Moor, South Dartmoor, Devon

above right

Odd thing, photographing ones own drink, but at least it shows the brown oil-clothed table at The Rugglestone Inn

Everyone drank the Plymouth Bass. Except me, a know-all from Leicestershire who couldn't understand why there was no Newcastle Brown. After my first three weeks I called in at six o'clock and as I lifted the latch I heard the simply wonderful landlady Audrey say from the pantry, 'Now I've got it you better drink it'. She had been seen earlier driving back from Plymouth with a stack of crates tied to the top of her black Morris Minor. I did drink most of it, getting into trouble for wanting to keep the empty bottles on the table. The balance was seen off by everyone on my last night. The round system was effortless as Audrey ran about bringing the beer to the tables. A pint would be thrust into your hand and she'd whisper in your ear, 'That's with Gerry,' and you'd wink across at Gerry and he'd wink back. Later you'd say to her *sotto voce*, 'And one for Gerry and Tom,' and it all happened in reverse. If you spilt beer on the floor a mop was thrust at you.

It took me about a month to decipher the Devon accents. Audrey laughed one night and said to me, 'You don't know what they're saying about you do you?'. At first I could only recognise 'bugger' but very soon these people became my friends; farmers who sat drinking with their backs to sheep sale posters attached to the tongue-and-groove wall, a huge haulier who sat in green overalls under a calendar

above left
A near perfect pub interior, The Compasses, Littley Green, Essex

above right
A 1920s' Bisto drum to hold matchsticks for The Rugglestone Inn's card games

advertising his Bovey Tracey fleet of lorries. One farmer came in every night and sat under the clock with a half pint to have with a sandwich he'd brought in his pocket. I think he may have worn leather gaiters.

At an unseen signal Audrey would lift up the brown oilcloth and get out playing cards and cribbage boards for a game I could never fathom. (I think it was called 'euchre'.) The dead matches used for counters were kept in a vintage Bisto drum, and every night Audrey, knowing my predilections, would see me looking at it and say, 'You can keep your hands off'. On my last night we all finished off the Newcastle Brown and sang songs very loudly. As I went out the door Audrey lifted up the cloth, took out the Bisto drum, emptied the matches out into the drawer and said, 'Here. You better have this I suppose.'

above
Oil lamp and Gold Flake mirror at the Falkland Arms

top right
Falkland Arms, Great Tew, Oxfordshire

bottom right
Windsor Castle, Notting Hill, London

Windsor Castle and Falkland Arms

Public houses like The Rugglestone were once common, chiefly in the countryside but always with city counterparts if you knew where to look. The trouble is we don't know where we are anymore. Because so many pubs are now owned by doubtful chains and put a new manager in every week they just become an impersonal business like a branch of Currys. And have their names changed to something stupid like the Holepunch and Zebra. Favourite pubs tend now to be favourite pubs in particular years; The Blue Ball in 1976, The Clifton in 1988, The Doves in 1994. The really good ones, though, are the ones that haven't even painted the ceiling for twenty years or, if they're really clever, have painted it but made it look as if they haven't. So the best always seem to be those that don't appear to change anything except the barrels, whatever else happens. Here's a handful that I hope are still there and as I first saw them.

There's a pub in Notting Hill called Windsor Castle because apparently before the ugly block of flats were built opposite you could actually see Windsor Castle from the windows. The front bar has a sloping wooden floor that means if you spill your beer it runs very slowly in a stream

down towards the counter. (If there's more than one stream you can bet on which will get there first.) You reach the gents by going out into Campden Hill and round the corner into Peel Street, and it's got the old Charringtons' name

Old Neptune, Whitstable

outside in metal letters under a mantle of greenery. As they say on their matchbox, this is a country pub in the heart of London.

The Falkland Arms in Great Tew, Oxfordshire still produces contented sighs. Oil lamps, an inglenook fireplace, flagstone floors, an original Gold Flake mirror and a rack of clay pipes and tobacco jars next to the bar. From the stone mullioned windows one can see the early nineteenth-century planting by John Claudius Loudon moving against the yellowy-brown building stone and village children running about in the school playground. It's all so English you feel that very soon an orchestra will start playing George Butterworth's *Banks of Green Willow.*

The seaside is well served by the Old Neptune in Whitstable, Kent. This weatherboarded pub sits right on the shingle amongst the coloured boats. No pretence here, you come in, get your beer and sit in the bay windows drinking and staring wistfully out at it all like a retired sea captain. Odd chairs and tables, a chalked blackboard giving a hint of food and the strange feeling that on a storm-tossed night the door might fly open and characters from a Charles Dickens novel might burst in with flurries of salt spray and lay out a drowned sailor on the wooden floorboards.

Queen's Head, Newton, Cambridgeshire

Pier Hotel, Harwich, Essex

Victoria, Eastleach, Gloucestershire

The Salutation, Norham, Northumberland

Kirkstone Pass Inn, Cumbria

Haven Inn, Boston, Lincolnshire

nnia, Dungeness, Kent

The Trip to Jerusalem, Nottingham

n Stars, Carey Street, London

The Anchor, Sutton Gault, Cambridgeshire

King's Head, Laxfield, Suffolk

Old Neptune, Whitstable, Kent

Hundreds of breweries and brands have vanished almost without trace, but their ghosts still cling on to the walls of countless pubs:

opposite clockwise from top left
Lyddington, Rutland; Norwich, Norfolk; Gravesend, Kent; Blackfriars, London; Northmoor, Oxfordshire; Stow-on-the-Wold, Gloucestershire

Seven Stars and Philharmonic

below left
Philharmonic, Hope Street, Liverpool

below right
Seven Stars, Carey Street, London

Seven Stars in Carey Street, London is a survivor that hides behind the Law Courts on the Strand. A true survivor because it managed to avoid being burned down in the Great Fire of 1666 and has just celebrated its 400th birthday. Everything round here is steeped in pink-ribboned legalese of some sort: law bookshops, solicitors' practices, barristers' chambers and scurrying figures in gowns and wigs. This is their

refreshment bar, a place for a quick pint with herrings or oysters between cases, the alternating smiles and frowns of celebration and commiseration. The walls have posters on

them for films like the 1937 *Action for Slander* and a precipitous staircase leads up to the toilets. Only a pub like this could have a landlady called Roxy Beaujolais, only someone with her tenacity could have kept a pub like this as it is.

Walk between the two Liverpool cathedrals and you will find yourself on Hope Street. On the opposite corner to the Philharmonic Hall is the Philharmonic Hotel, (*built* 1898–1900) and if you like completely over-the-top Victoriana, then this is the one for you. Walter Thomas was the man responsible, the architect for local brewer Robert Cain, and he pulled every possible trick out of his bag of decorative devices. Richly-patterned wallpapers, glossy majolica tiles, frosted lamps, stained-glass ceiling lights, it's all here. Much of the woodwork was crafted by joiners when laid off from working on the great Transatlantic liners down on the Mersey shipyards. This is a great pub for that mid-afternoon drink when you should be doing something else, sunlight seeping through and reflecting off the rows of polished beer pumps. And, if all this isn't quite enough, the toilets are done out in Twyford's Rouge Royale.

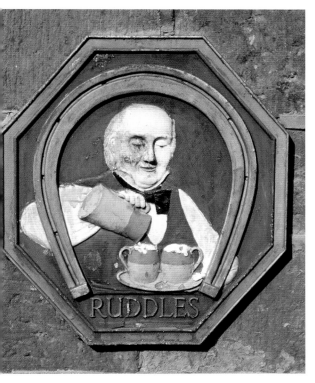

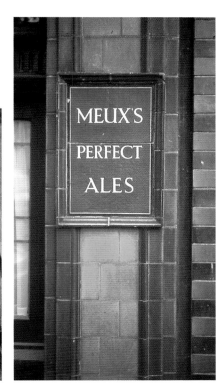

STATION TO STATION

No more will I go to Blandford Forum and Mortehoe
On the slow train from Midsomer Norton and Mumby Road.
No churns, no porter, no cat on a seat
At Chorlton-cum-Hardy or Chester-le-Street.

'The Slow Train', Michael Flanders and Donald Swann

opposite
A John Smith's pub sign illustrated by Andrew Davidson and realised in vitreous enamel on steel

Blandford Forum in Dorset closed in 1966; Mortehoe, tucked up in North Devon, in 1970. Mumby Road was the station of my childhood holidays on the Lincolnshire coast, where a big Austin taxi waited outside to take us across the green marsh to a line of bungalows sitting on the sand dunes like a row of deckchairs. The only reminder of the station now is a red-brick tile-hung house next to a shadowy trace in the grass that was once known to railwaymen as the Louth, Mablethorpe and Willoughby Loop. Flanders and Swann's milk churns, porters and cats on seats are now folklore, the stuff of nostalgic musings of a halcyon past that might also include such platform impedimenta as pigeons in wicker baskets and big red Berkel weighing machines.

At best, the railway station today is a 'retail opportunity', with city termini disguised as shopping malls in which trains just happen to arrive and depart somewhere behind the franchises; well-thumbed Bradshaw Railway Guides replaced by the banalities of customer care manuals. At worst it will be a vandalised plastic bus shelter shivering on the remains of a Victorian platform, a far whistle from the gas-lit halt with sweet briar twisting round the name board. Occasionally we may still catch fragments of a more leisured past. Acme Thunderer whistles shrieking up to the roof spandrels of William Peachey's York; the hanging baskets being watered at Settle with its Midland crimson lake paintwork and barge-boarded gable ends. Or perhaps the near-perfect atmosphere of stone-built Stamford, with the 1848 gilded weathervane catching the sunlight on its airy octagonal turret.

But now we will usually only enjoy these pleasures in the cardboard dreams of meticulously-detailed model railways, or in the mementoes on preserved steam railways where the past is kept as freshly-painted as a row of fire buckets. Staverton in Devon still proudly displays milk churns on a trolley, metal soldiers eternally on parade for the early morning milk train that will never again shuffle alongside the Dart from Buckfastleigh, whilst in the sidings doze a camping coach and a dusty pink example of a Hornby favourite, the Royal Daylight oil wagon.

We can never completely recapture the spirit of the past, but there is now something of a railway rennaissance in terms of architecture. Although the trains themselves may have windows that don't open and mindless detergent packet-style liveries, the buildings they visit are in many cases enjoying a spruceness unseen since their brass band inaugural openings in Victoria's England. Ketton stone and Stewartby brick is being hosed down to lift off the ingrained carapaces of engine soot, cupolas are pigeon-proofed and long-forgotten cast-iron railway heraldry is once again paint-box bright.

opposite
Stamford, Lincolnshire

top left
Staverton, Devon

top right
Hellifield, North Yorkshire

But that's only for the survivors. Hundreds more have disappeared forever into the black holes engineered by successive ill-advised bureaucrats and their self-serving political masters. At the height of the railway system in Britain, nobody was more than 12 miles from a station. Even in the remote fastnesses of the Yorkshire Dales the mournful whistles of Midland locomotives could be heard echoing around the arches of monumental viaducts that brought trim red carriages under the glass and iron canopies of Hellifield, alongside the *cottage orné* of Settle and then out across unpredictable heavy country up to Horton-in-Ribblesdale and what was once England's highest mainline station at Dent, recently sold off. Amazingly though, the whistles are still heard on the Settle to Carlisle line, thanks to the endeavours of those who fought so valiantly for its survival.

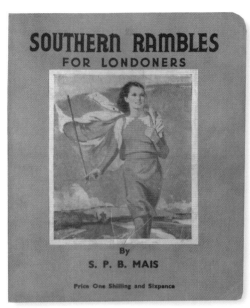

Southern Style

Most of us were much nearer to our local station. London's commuter destinations survived more than most, particularly those serving the home counties of Kent, Surrey and Sussex. Between the wars this was Southern country, the only one of the railway companies incorporated in the 'Big Four' in 1923 whose lines did not venture out of England. Their electric trains brought home the bowler-hatted officers of commerce to their pre-prandial gin and tonics. 'He's something in the City,' was the watchword at Sunday lunchtime cocktails in Dorking, Cuckfield, Fawkham-cum-Hartley. By their immaculately-rolled umbrellas shall ye know them. These were companions-of-honour that shared compartments of regular trains, their attaché cases in parade-ground order on string luggage racks, clattering over the points as they wound out of Victoria or Waterloo into the evening light. The weekday club around which H.E. Bates's short stories often unfold; the memorable opening scene of Tony Hancock's film *The Rebel*.

And it wasn't only commuters arriving and departing in the station yards. At the weekends the ebb and flow from London reversed, and the station names were looked out for by

London's leisure seekers. Ramblers, hikers, walkers, what you will, all egged-on by the Southern Railway's sixpenny pocket guides, written by the astonishingly prolific S.P.B. Mais with titles like *Let's Get Out Here*. And get out they did, not just in the Southern's immediate home-land, but also as far afield as Salisbury, Exeter, anywhere on the route of the Atlantic Express.

The beautiful covers were in a hardy simulated leather finish with glued-on picture labels, two of them, *Let's Get Out Here* and *Walks in North Devon* illustrated by Audrey Weber. Her style brought something of the hotly exotic to the Southern; England as appealing as the continent the railway served through south coast ports.

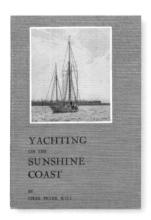

above
Southern Railway's *Yachting on the Sunshine Coast* was written by Charles Pears and illustrated with his superb maritime watercolours, all orientated around the Southern's coastal stations

right and opposite
Southern Railway guides, all by the prolific S.P.B. Mais, describing walks and rambles within easy reach of their stations

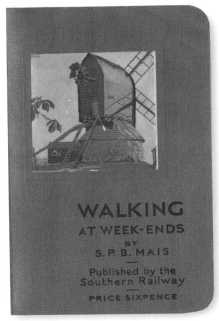

WALKING
AT WEEK-ENDS
BY
S. P. B. MAIS
—
Published by the
Southern Railway
—
PRICE SIXPENCE

WALKS IN
NORTH DEVON
BY S. P. B. MAIS
6ᵈ Published by the
Southern Railway

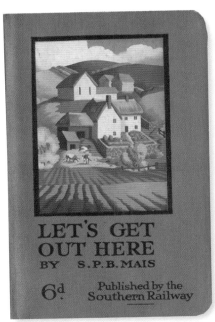

LET'S GET
OUT HERE
BY S. P. B. MAIS
6ᵈ Published by the
Southern Railway

The company made an intriguing disclaimer in the guides: '… the Southern Railway is unable to accept responsibility for any loss or prejudice arising through any mis-statements or inaccuracies contained therein.' I wonder what instigated that? Probably an incident with a moleskinned gamekeeper or an outraged bull, pipes and maps flying through the air. The back cover of *Walking at Weekends* had an advertisement for Vick's Vapour-Rub for quick relief from, amongst a host of other things 'Headaches, Bruises, Scratches…'

SOUTHERN RAMBLES
KENT
S. P. B. MAIS
1/6

York

Settle, North Yorkshire

Oakham, Rutland

Harlow Town, Essex

Great Malvern, Worcestershire

Sleaford, Lincolnshire

rton, Devon

Salisbury, Wiltshire

s Cross, London

Hellifield, North Yorkshire

ster

Cromford, Derbyshire

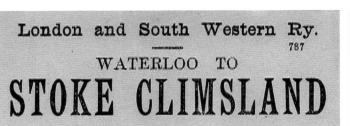

London and South Western Ry. 787

WATERLOO TO

STOKE CLIMSLAND

G. E. R.

Aldeburgh

E.R.O. 21556/132

LMS

(12/46)
6M.

SOUTHERN RAILWAY

(787)

FROM WATERLOO TO

WINCHFIELD

G. W. R.

Oakengates

(8/49)
6M.

BRITISH RAILWAYS

(787)

FROM WATERLOO TO

STRAWBERRY HILL

L. & N. W. RY.

Dawlish

Est. 4772 5M. 8/37

B 877

L. N E. R.

LUGGAGE

From YORK

To **WHITBY**

45809

G. E. R.

From

TO

ALDEBURGH

SOUTHERN RAILWAY.

787

FROM WATERLOO TO

CRYSTAL PALACE

(Via Clapham Junc.)

opposite
A gazetteer of railway England on paper luggage labels with a 1930s' Hornby O Gauge porter

top left and right
The Southern Railway style on the Watercress Line in Hampshire, with a signal box and topiary at Alresford station

top bottom right
Emergency services at Horsted Keynes in East Sussex

Southern Railway stations were as green as the woods and fields through which their slam-door trains hummed. 'Mid Chrome Green' the paint swatch called it, and it was lavished on drain pipes, valance mouldings, awning columns, railings, handrails, window frames, doors. And lamp posts. A shade of green that survived nationalisation in 1948 to brand the totem station signs for what became the Southern Region of British Railways. The other regions also received their colours: orange for the North West, pale blue for Scotland, a deep burgundy for the Midlands. I started to associate them with their different geographies so much so that I invented a curious and wildly inaccurate mythology for them: the Southern was obviously downland, the Western Region matched brown cows and clotted cream, and the Eastern had a deep navy blue to represent the North Sea of its coastal fringes. But whatever the reasons for the choices, there was an unerring sense of permanence, pride, confidence. Here to stay, we assumed.

If you want to see how it all used to be, take a look at Horsted Keynes on the Bluebell Line in Sussex where they even have a Southern coffin carrier, a suitably hearse-like adaptation of a luggage trolley. The entire station has been preserved as a classic example of Southern style, complete with details like stacked-up luggage and an original Nestlé's chocolate vending machine.

Trackside Style

right
An Airfix plastic model kit
modelled on Oakham's
signal box

opposite
A May morning in Dorset
as a GWR local train
steams through the
Waddon Vale between
Abbotsbury and Upwey

bottom
Hornby tin signal box

There was also much to see between the
stations. The line-side telegraph poles created
the illusion that they were only there to stop
the wires from continually attempting to curve
ever upwards to the sky; the train itself
shadowed on fields flecked with broken clouds
of white smoke from the engine. We had an
innate sense of security on seeing signalmen
watching the train go by from boxes, knowing

that they were masters of the track with their
heavy signal and point levers pulled with the
aid of a bit of cotton waste, the block
instruments with their twitching indicators,
brass bells and telephones ringing out. (So
much more reassuring than computer
monitors watched 60 miles away in a room
with no windows.)

The look of a signal box followed a similar
pattern all over the country. The design
developed over seventy years from the 1860s: a
timber and glass operational deck over a brick
ground floor, gable ends often finished off with
decorative bargeboards and Gothic finials, and
a little railed walkway facilitating the essential
cleaning of the windows. Oakham level crossing
box in Rutland's county town was so archetypical
it was used as the template for the Airfix plastic
construction kit for model railways.

right
Wansford, Cambridgeshire

below right
A signal hut at Coombe
Junction, Cornwall

below left
Signalman's lavatory and
coal store at Culgaith,
Cumbria

Inside the signal box was a cornucopia of coloured levers and mahogany instruments for the business of seeing a train safely through the section, the comforts evolving around a coal or coke fire, a big aluminium kettle and a sturdy leather armchair dragged out from a refurbished waiting room. The floor was always spotlessly clean, the clock regularly checked and maintained. In 1900 there were 13,000 signal boxes, now there are fewer than 1,000. If you want to see just how atmospheric they can be, get hold of the little film made of Charles Dickens's 'The Signalman', but don't watch it just before you go to bed.

Level crossings were once very heavy wooden gates painted white with a big red disc in the middle and an oil lamp positioned on top. A few years ago when I was sent out by Railtrack to photograph anything that appealed to me on their vast estate, I discovered many of these original gates still opened and closed by signalmen or even by ladies living in adjacent cottages. Not so long before this expedition I came across one chap sitting in a corrugated-iron hut with a mug of Lemsip in one hand and an LNER pocket watch in the other. As we go to press Frinton-on-Sea (q.v.) is about to lose its crossing gates and human being, so desperate are they to get rid of it all in favour of a CCTV camera.

Platelayers' huts (somewhere for tea to be brewed in a billycan, a pipe to be smoked in peace) have all but disappeared. Survivors include a succession of concrete huts out on the mainlines south west from Waterloo, prefabricated and with chamfered roof lines, Art Deco utility from the Southern again. Everything one saw on the railways, from the largest termini stations and express trains down to the smallest signal box and guard's whistle appeared to have a rightness of purpose about it, a visual appeal that came from function rather than from cosmetic styling.

Now the railways change with alarming regularity as the franchises come and go; indeed much of the original infrastructure has been made obsolete. We don't need lamp huts – where the station junior filled lanterns with oil – anymore, and waiting rooms just for ladies must seem slightly old-fashioned, however appealing. But it's sad that the intimate personal knowledge of a train's whereabouts has been turned into indifferent digitised displays, the coalyards into car parks and refreshment buffets into Olde Grizzler's Pastie Co. And perhaps worst of all, now that ticket pricing has become so ludicrously complicated and meaningless, is the fact that we don't have ticket collectors anymore, only passenger-threatening 'Revenue Protection Officers'.

Railway of Life

It wasn't all perfect of course. There was soot in
the eyes, dry rot in the buffet sandwiches. Trains
could be just as late as they are now ('Listen Sir,
how can it be late when it's been cancelled?') and
carriages were often either freezing cold or horribly tropical. But there was something about the
trains, and even more about the stations, that was
almost indefinable. I think it was because they
were part of the soul of the community, scenes of
joyous arrival and sad departure. A fixed point
like the parish church and its vicar, who was
invariably a railway buff banging on about the
railway of life. Vintage television's *All Gas and
Gaiters* with Derek Nimmo, William Mervyn and
Robertson Hare as clergymen planning fictional
train journeys with railway guides and stop-
watches. Booking hall timetables, hymn numbers on the chancel arch. Waiting room posters
promising sun-filled holidays, Sunday school
posters of the Promised Land. No wonder the
railway revolution quickly picked up on the
Gothic Revival, turning stations into hymns of
praise. Great Malvern with its cut-out iron vegeta-
tion on the awning columns, Battle in Sussex like
an Early English monastery. Even the 1991 brick
towers at Liverpool Street appear to be an echo
of Southwell Minster.

I learnt about railway stations from a very early age. My grandfather opted out of the army before the Great War (good move) in order to work for the Midland Railway at Wellingborough. This was a red brick and stone station designed in 1857 by C.H. Driver and built on the eastern extremities of this typical Northamptonshire boot-and-shoe town on the River Nene. A cinder path ran up from the station yard to quiet streets of equally red-brick terraced houses where my grandparents lived.

They had an outside lavatory that proudly displayed a recently obsolete copy of an ABC Railway Guide hanging by baler twine on the back of the door. At 636 pages long it was a very early example of paper recycling, in use as both obscure reading material and as a novel alternative to the toilet roll.

We travelled from Wigston Magna station (closed 1968) in Leicestershire to Wellingborough every Good Friday to see my grandmother and her Brobdignagian Yorkshire Puddings. (They swam in gravy like 'Madagascar in the Indian Ocean', as Dennis Potter once described spotted dick and custard.) The journey was only a matter of some 30 miles, but the little steam train stopped at no less than seven stations.

All were in the *cottage orné* Midland style, typified by lozenge-shaped glazing in the windows and stone dressings to the brickwork. We stepped out on to the platform at Wellingborough under a glass and iron canopy that was crammed with ornamented floral curliques, a very tangible sense of arrival with the slamming of doors, porters' shouts as they unloaded parcels on to big hand barrows and guards' whistles blowing.

Our departure was always after the gas lamps had been lit by the simple expedient of pulling thin chains down from the fittings, and I think our arrival at the station was timed early so that we could see a couple of expresses shriek through. My father would stand with his back to a banked-up coal fire in the booking hall, chatting to one of my grandfather's successors. He shared out his bag of Brazil nut toffees and I stared at a poster for Butlin's on the wall behind him, slightly disturbed at the sight of an air-brushed girl holding aloft a brightly-coloured beach ball. What had she got to do with Butlin's? As much as Philip Larkin's white-satined girl had to do with 'Sunny Prestatyn' I suspect.

Once, when our train clanked in, my father spoke to the guard and for some reason I travelled back to Wigston Magna in the guard's van. Parcels were thrown in and out at the intervening stations, the highlight coming at Glendon & Rushton when something big and squashy in a sack was thrown in, sounding like a bag of wet liver hitting the wooden floorboards of the van. A card label attached to the sack said 'Harboro / Glue Factory'. 'What's that?' I asked. The guard started the train off and slammed his window up. 'Dead dog,' he replied cheerfully. Now we really won't see the likes of that again.

THE OPEN ROAD

THE OPEN ROAD

opposite
Detail from a 1925 Ordnance Survey map cover designed by Ellis Martin for the 10-mile map of Britain

You don't hear anybody saying 'Let's take to the open road' much these days. Perhaps because the experience of driving in England in the early twenty-first century can be such a depressing business. The roads are not so much 'open' as clogged with thousands of lorries taking oven chips from Felixstowe to Rugby and then back to Felixstowe again, and cars all desperate to get to the tanning salon or next retail park. There is far too much road signing, much of it abysmal in design, and to make matters worse the fields at the sides of motorways are now full of posters for things like self-adhesive labels. Even country roads can't be left alone, with wind-powered 'Slow Down' signs, dreadful smears of coloured paint on the road surfaces and 'Traffic Calming Measures' that make even the most mild-mannered driver want to kill something. On a very rural 8-mile stretch of the A43 in Northamptonshire there are over 150 signs, including a batch warning of speed cameras that aren't actually there.

Of course right-thinking folk once got enraged just at the thought of there being cars on the road at all ('They'll frighten the horses'), and the government made a man walk in front of them waving a red flag. But as the twentieth century got into gear and traffic increased beyond a couple of Darraques and a Panhard-Levassor so too roadside furniture developed. We needed to know about sharp bends, T-junctions and whether or not we were likely to be side-swiped by a steam train on an ungated level crossing, so traffic signs evolved. Our new cars required petrol so filling 'stations' opened and, as we were always 'gasping for a cuppa', roadside cafés got out the gingham tablecloths. Blacksmiths turned into garages, ex-sergeant majors into AA patrolmen. The driving gloves were drawn on, the mirror adjusted. Motoring started to put its foot down.

Milestones

Milestones were something of a curiosity to the new motorist. They are a relic of the coaching era, but first introduced by the Romans on their military roads only to disappear until the eighteenth century when Trinity Hall installed a series marked with their crescent on what is now the B1368 in Cambridgeshire. With the advent of Turnpike Acts a splendid variety of designs appeared, each with a vernacular flavour: the naïve letterforms on western markers that echo local standing stones, durable cast iron in the North weathering all storms with crisp legible characters. All now under threat as councils remove them to make the mowing easier, the unscrupulous steal them and the rest sink into oblivion in ditches and undergrowth. But in places they are surviving, and there's a Milestone Society to help them stand their ground.

*I wish, by the way, that I had noted down more
of the names on the signboards at the cross-roads*

The South Country, Edward Thomas

Signposts

Signposts have survived in far greater numbers than milestones, perhaps because we really do need them, no matter what our SatNavs tell us. But the traditional designs are under threat, sadly all too often replaced by penny-pinching subsitutes with computer-generated letters on reflective backgrounds. Happily this isn't always the case. Dorset religiously maintains its posts, which are surmounted by the county roundel and show the local parish, and have even kept the unique Red Post near Anderson, a reminder of the marker put here to guide illiterate soldiers marching convicts to Portsmouth for transportation. The road junction is a day's march from Dorchester Gaol, and the Red Post indicated the turning to the aptly-named Botany Bay Farm, the first night's stop-over. Rutland keeps its signposts in immaculate condition, re-painting the timber structures regularly and re-fixing metal letters that are still made specifically for the job. The maintenance crew out on Rutland's roads will tell you it's just the best job to have in the summer.

Originally finger posts, some at a height to ease the reading of them by coachmen up on their high seats, they became more formalised in design after the Parliamentary Acts of 1766

and 1773 made them compulsory. As traffic increased a system of road numbering was introduced and signposts proliferated. Invasion fears in the Second World War saw them removed and put into storage for the duration.

Once you try and design a signpost, to tack on 'improvements' like spuriously-named footpath indicators, they fail. The best signposts look as good as they do, and are at home in their environment, simply because they have evolved slowly through their basic function, to just put us on the right road for our destination.

opposite
High summer in Seaton, Rutland

above
Signpost near Fotheringhay, Northamptonshire

right
Detail from the cover for hotel guide *Let's Halt Awhile* (1935)

Brooke, Norfolk

Yoxford, Suffolk

Lyndon, Rutland

Deddington, Oxfordshire

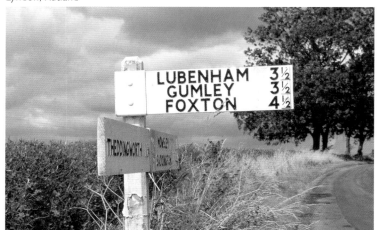

Laughton Hills, Leicestershire

Holywell, Lincolnshire

...ed, Essex

Rampisham, Dorset

...rson, Dorset

Burton Park, West Sussex

...ash, East Sussex

Aydon, Northumberland

Road Signs

below
Belisha card game

right
Loddington, Leicestershire
and a warning for a
Double Corner

opposite
Road signs from a gentler
era. All but the Belisha
beacon and school sign
are thoughtfully preserved
examples found at Horsted
Keynes station on the
Bluebell Line in East Sussex

Original road signs fell to continental influences comparatively early, so it is now very rare to find extant examples. The 1930s' Highway Codes only gave nine variations, including the stentorian 'Halt at Major Road Ahead' with its red triangle in a circle, although as the illustrations were only in black it had to be annotated as 'signal red'. The same editions still had the rules on how to use your horse whip for hand signals. The arrival of the motorway put paid to all that; the existing system of road signs simply couldn't cope so designers Jock Kinneir and Margaret Calvert were commissioned to create the signs for the first motorway, the M6 Preston bypass. The Worboys Committee of 1963 followed recommendations to adopt the European standard, particularly as these would obviate the need for a driver to know English in order to understand their meaning.

The mandatory red circles and red warning triangles with their simple wording became highway folklore along with drophead Sunbeam and saluting AA patrols. The stuff of a gentler countryside, the friendly wagging finger of admonishment rather than the crassness of money-grabbing speed cameras hiding behind mantras about road safety. I particularly liked the two signs warning of the likelihood of children suddenly bouncing balls or school-books into the road, a Ladybird-book innocence realised in scissorcut silhouettes. Only the Belisha beacon still flashes with matey winks, the brilliant initiative of Leslie Hore-Belisha, Minister of Transport in 1935. So popular was the idea Pepys brought out a Belisha card game that educated children about road signs in general, part of the new Safety First campaign.

Motor Cars

They needed Mr Universe muscles to steer them, could be hell to start and suffered from indifferent brakes. But like the old codger who leaks beer into the carpet down the pub, the motor car was once full of genuine character. I bought the Riley pictured opposite in 1972, only seventeen years after it was built in Abingdon-on-Thames, next to the MG factory. After the Mini Moke I had hared about in this was sheer luxury. Red leather seats, a wooden dashboard, a nifty click-click sort of gearbox. And the original valve radio, which meant that when it finally warmed up out came Variety Bandbox. It had instant appeal for me, having seen the marque as a child while I car-spotted with my grubby *Observer's Book of Automobiles*. And yes, the traffic was worth looking at. Morris Oxfords with menacing radiator grilles, razor-styled Triumph Renowns and Mayflowers, fat Austin Somersets and hump-backed Standard Vanguards. We didn't have a car at this time so I would go three doors away and ask if I could sit in my friend's dad's black Morris 10 in order to make engine noises. Or hang about looking lost in the middle of the road so that a neighbour would pick me up in his Humber Hawk, also black. (Imagine doing that now.) Traffic really

did have an immense visual appeal. A bright yellow Seddon brewery dray delivered Holes Newark Ales to the pub at the bottom of the road, the laundry was delivered in brown wrapping paper by a green and cream Morris Commercial with snowdrops painted on the doors. Dustbins were tipped out into a Shelvoke & Drewry and the Sunday joint brought by a three-wheel James Samson Handyvan. A Mazda was a light bulb.

opposite clockwise from top left
These we drove: Jaguar Mk2, Austin Devon pick-up. Bentley 'S' Series, Riley one and a half litre, Standard Vanguard Mk2, Wolseley 4/44 and who could resist driving a fire engine called Dennis?

left
Vanished names of a home-grown motor industry, once proud badges on quality motor cars. The Alvis name continues but only on military vehicles

Buses and Coaches

We have probably got used to the fact that cars appear to share the same designers as floor plans, and that every van is painted white and driven by somebody who wants to kill us, but what about how buses and coaches look? This is a very particular *bête noir* of mine, the rot having set in with the unfathomable National Bus Company in the early 1970s, whose slogan was 'Together We Can Really Go Places'. Up to that point we appeared to have bus companies in smart liveries as individual as the locations they moved in. Like railway station signs, they were an indicator that we had travelled some distance from home. Red was used for Devon General, Yorkshire Traction, Eastern Counties and of course the Midland Red; maroon and cream East Kents parked next to green and cream Southdowns in Victoria Coach Station.

above
Liveries for Maidstone & District and Southdown buses

right
A 1930s' clockwork Greenline toy coach

Corporations were proud to fly the colours of municipal service: mid-blue for Birkenhead, dark blue for Birmingham, yellow and green for Halifax. Identities were equally reassuring: Leicester's heraldic fleur-de-lys city badge, Maidstone & District's logo swirls formed to include the description 'motor services', Southdown's confident signature flourish, Nottinghamshire's Barton Transport sporting a banner-waving Robin Hood. London Transport kept it simple, with classic logotypes in gold, on red for urban services, green for country buses. The National Bus Company started the trend of making buses look like badly-designed cigarette packs, even forcing Black & White of Cheltenham to suffer the indignity of having their name painted in red and blue. But it's got much, much worse. Mediocre laptop presentations are blown up to cover vehicles with trashy graphics and meaningless slogans;

hideous advertising covers entire buses. Local identity and civic pride have vanished in clouds of filthy exhaust smoke. But whilst we can't live in an hermetically-sealed *Heartbeat* existence, I think it's time we gave the same consideration to public service vehicles that we give to buildings. After all, some of them are as big as houses.

Garages

above left
Much Marcle, Herefordshire

above centre
Willingham, Cambridgeshire

above right
Stockbridge, Hampshire

opposite
Christmas at the Holly & Ivy

right
BP and National Benzole
badges

There was a time when BP stood for British Petroleum and the man in overalls who filled your car with petrol was very likely the garage mechanic. We called them garages then, but now they're all 'services' and apparently they make more money on a Mars bar than on a gallon of petrol. So, the traditional garage with a couple of pumps and someone to change a spark plug is gradually disappearing. In 1967 we had 40,000 petrol stations, now it's around 8,000. And the little local garage simply can't compete with sterile supermarket-style services that would rather sell you wilting flowers in stifling cellophane to leave at road accidents than have someone check your oil or tyres. Bring back greasy rags, Castrol dispensers, feet sticking out from under oil sumps and sharp intakes of breath.

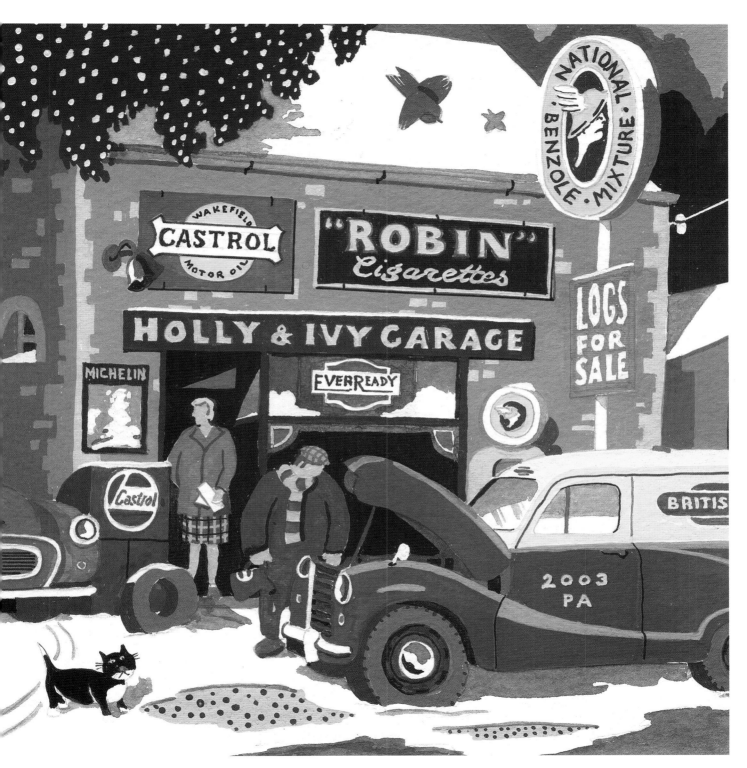

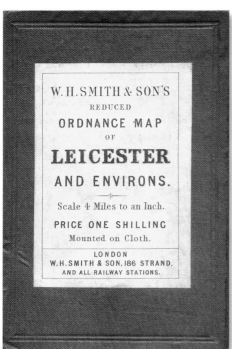

W. H. SMITH & SON'S
REDUCED
ORDNANCE MAP
OF
LEICESTER
AND ENVIRONS.

Scale 4 Miles to an Inch.

PRICE ONE SHILLING
Mounted on Cloth.

LONDON
W. H. SMITH & SON, 186 STRAND.
AND ALL RAILWAY STATIONS.

ORDNANCE SURVEY
10-MILE MAP OF
GREAT BRITAIN
IN THREE SHEETS
SHEET 3
Price 5/- Net.

G R
Published by the Ordnance Survey Office
SOUTHAMPTON

E R

ORDNANCE SURVEY OF GREAT BRITAIN

"QUARTER-INCH" MAP
FOURTH EDITION

ENGLAND, NORTH-EAST

SHEET 3

Price—Three Shillings

PUBLISHED BY THE DIRECTOR GENERAL
ORDNANCE SURVEY
SOUTHAMPTON

164

NATIONAL GRID   SEVENTH SERIES

ORDNANCE
SURVEY

ONE-INCH MAP
of
GREAT BRITAIN

MINEHEAD

Price (Paper) Five Shillings & Sixpence Net

Sheet 164

FULLY REVISED   PUBLISHED
1957-58   1960

ORDNANCE SURVEY "ONE-INCH" MAP

Dorking & Leith Hill
Mounted on Linen
Price Three Shillings

Published by the Ordnance Survey Office, Southampton

Practical Motorist

Principal ROAD ROUTES *of* Great Britain

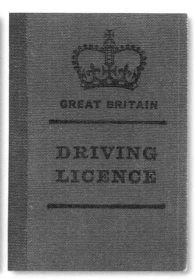

GREAT BRITAIN

DRIVING LICENCE

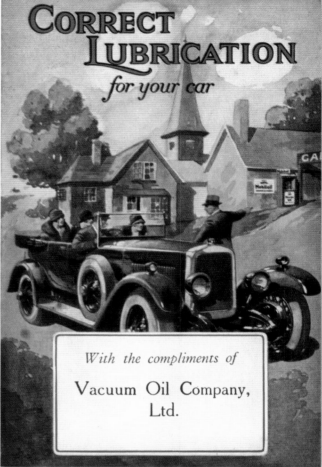

CORRECT LUBRICATION *for your car*

With the compliments of

Vacuum Oil Company, Ltd.

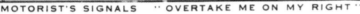

MOTORIST'S SIGNALS " OVERTAKE ME ON MY RIGHT "

WILL'S'S CIGARETTES

Ministry of Transport

THE HIGHWAY CODE

Issued by the Minister of Transport with the Authority of Parliament

(WITH SUPPLEMENTARY NOTES)

Crown Copyright Reserved

LONDON
PUBLISHED BY HIS MAJESTY'S STATIONERY OFFICE
Price 1d. Net

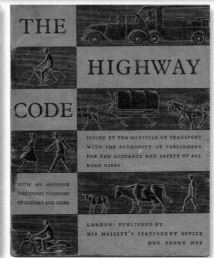

THE HIGHWAY CODE

ISSUED BY THE MINISTER OF TRANSPORT WITH THE AUTHORITY OF PARLIAMENT FOR THE GUIDANCE AND SAFETY OF ALL ROAD USERS

WITH AN APPENDIX INCLUDING DIAGRAMS OF SIGNALS AND SIGNS

LONDON: PUBLISHED BY HIS MAJESTY'S STATIONERY OFFICE
ONE PENNY NET

THE HIGHWAY CODE

HER MAJESTY'S STATIONERY OFFICE · PRICE 1d NET

THE HIGHWAY CODE
INCLUDING MOTORWAY RULES

HER MAJESTY'S STATIONERY OFFICE · PRICE 6d NET

ENGLAND BY THE SEA

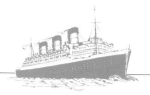

We do love to be beside the seaside. The constant draw of the coast means that we are never happier than when paddling, digging, lying in the sun or just staring at it all. We have our favourite spots. Often this will be beaches favoured by a few thousand others, but we can be equally happy alone on remote cliff tops where we can be just ourselves. The coastline is of course as varied as we are, catering for all tastes, catering for no taste at all or, mostly, just being the coast of England without regard to anybody.

Nowhere in England is very far from the sea. Even the most land-locked towns are less than a hundred miles away, making coastal resorts easily accessible even for a day out. Manchester rushes out to Blackpool, Newcastle to Whitley Bay. Middlesbrough has Redcar, Leeds and Bradford have Bridlington and Scarborough. Nottingham and Leicester head for Skegness or Great Yarmouth, and London is particularly spoilt for choice, being on the corner of England as it were. The Thames becomes the Essex and North Kent coasts, the south coast becomes London-by-the-Sea with Hastings, Eastbourne, Brighton, Bognor Regis. And then there are all the bits in between: wide open bleak Northumberland, the great sea curve of Norfolk and Suffolk, downland chalk sliced through to make the vertiginous cliffs of Sussex and Dorset, the secret coves of the West Country hiding below fog-bound moors.

In the early 1970s the BBC made a remarkable film in their Bird's Eye View series. Aerial photography showed the east coast from the Tweed to London's Tower Bridge, with a commentary by Gordon Jackson. The idea was irresistible, so I've adapted it to give a lightning tour of the English coast between the cast iron lighthouses of Berwick-on-Tweed in Northumberland and Maryport in Cumbria.

Berwick to Beadnell

For most of the medieval period Berwick-on-Tweed passed back and forth between England and Scotland like a shuttlecock. At the moment it's in England, the border River Tweed making one last twist around the town before decanting into the North Sea. Berwick is more of a riverside town than seaside, but we're left in no doubt as to where we are when we see the lighthouse, red-capped like some curious fungus at the end of the long curving stone pier.

The main Edinburgh to King's Cross line turns out at Berwick to hug the coastline past Redskin Cove and Saltpan Rocks and, before moving inland again, passengers are rewarded by a view of Holy Island, loosely attached to the shore by its frightening causeway. The road can quickly be covered by the racing tide; a little wooden hut on stilts acts as a refuge for those not heeding the tide tables. The island itself is memorable for Lindisfarne Priory and the Lutyens-restored castle on its cone of rock,

above left
Beadnell lime kilns

above right
Seahouses Quayside

top
Bamburgh Sector light,
Northumberland

but also look out for the old boats turned upside down to become fishermens' stores.

The massive sandstone block of Bamburgh Castle dominates the village on one side and commands the ocean on the other above the white levels of beach. The Bamburgh Sector lighthouse peeps over the rocks, a building with a face complete with the illusion of a *retroussé* nose created by the Trinity House coat-of-arms. Seahouses Harbour is peopled with black-suited divers as they struggle to put on yellow air tanks while lobsters half-heartedly struggle to get out of creels next to boats pulled-up on the slipway. Beadnell Harbour is littered with creels and nets too, stored now in the remains of the unmissable eighteenth-century lime kilns grouped on the harbour, a reminder of past industry where limestone was burnt. The original kiln was expected to cough up a thousand cartloads of lime a year. On my first visit a woman running the little local shop stared at me and said, 'What lime kilns?'.

Snook Point to Spurn Head

The natural features of the Northumberland coast continue: Snook Point, Football Hole, Jenny Bells Carr. Embleton Bay sweeps round to the jagged remains of John of Gaunt's Dunstanburgh Castle. No car park here, just a bracing shoreline walk from Crabster. Pretty Alnmouth becomes a living LNER poster on its river estuary, Warkworth Castle and Amble look out to the lighthouse on Coquet Island. And then the pale orange smoke from Ashington's aluminium smelters and Blyth's incongruous string of wind turbines snaking out to sea announces Tyneside, a landscape relieved by Seaton Delaval Hall and St Mary's

Island with its tall white candle of a lighthouse.

A succession of more lighthouses marks the progression: the red tin man in white plimsolls standing on the Groin at South Shields, classic red and white stripes at Souter Point, and Roker marooned on its pleasant greensward. The outfalls of the Wear and the Tees break up the sprawl until at last it all thins out and we are in North Yorkshire and a wilder northeast facing coast punctuated by Staithes, Runswick Bay, Sandsend and Whitby. Here the spiky remains of the abbey haunt the clifftop, looking down over the fishing town with its St Mary's church, Dracula industry and the sepia toning of Frank

above left
The Rotunda,
Scarborough

above centre
Recycled lighthouse and
beach masonry, Spurn
Head

above right
Sunday television's
The Royal location,
Scarborough

Meadows Sutcliffe's photographs. And the Magpie restaurant with its big school posters of what fish look like before the hiss of the deep fryer.

Precipitous Robin Hood's Bay, wind-battered Ravenscar and then the manifold surprises of Scarborough. Henry II's castle built on top of a Roman signalling station, the truly grand 1867 Grand Hotel with its architectural mythology of 365 rooms and 'V' ground plan for Victoria. The Rotunda museum (another building with a face) below a vertiginous bridge, the warm jets of the French pavilion spa and finally the fanciful orange brick edifice on Holbeck Road that everybody knows as *The Royal* hospital on Sunday night television.

Filey, Flamborough Head, Bridlington. The long sweep down past Hornsea and Withernsea until Spurn Head hooks into the Humber. Along this shore it would seem the sea wants it all back; the storm surges and relentless waves suck everything away, dragging it southwards to spit it back at Lincolnshire. Half bungalows hanging off cliffs revealing flapping wallpapered interiors, tide-smoothed red brick amongst the shingle around Spurn's obsolete lighthouses.

Berwick-on-Tweed, Northumberland

Seahouses, Northumberland

South Gare, Redcar & Cleveland

Whitby, North Yorkshire

Flamborough, East Riding of Yorkshire

Southwold, Suffolk

ercourt, Essex

North Foreland, Kent

Watchet, Somerset

ham-on-Sea, Somerset

Black Nore, North Somerset

Fleetwood, Lancashire

Cleethorpes to Kings Lynn

Cleethorpes – Grimsby's seaside – stares out at the Hull ferries bound for Rotterdam and Zeebrugge as they leave the shelter of the Humber. And then another stretch of empty coast, so typical of England's eastern seaboard as Lincolnshire gains a new shore at the expense of Yorkshire. Danger area mudflats slowly build, leaving coastline villages lost: Tetney Haven, Somercotes Haven, Donna Nook. A previous coast can be traced a little way inland: North Cotes, Marshchapel, Grainthorpe, all on the marsh road that tips up in those odd depressing resorts of Mablethorpe and Sutton-on-Sea, equally marooned but this time by the loss of the railway that made them. Cut-price England: the home of the Pukka Pie from the hot cabinet, rock in the shape of poached eggs and shorts with plastic bums hanging out of them.

Anderby Creek, remote scene of my earliest holidays, is virtually unchanged. It still looks as if everything not tied down in a storm may suddenly take off in a crazy thrashing of electricity wires, later to land in Antwerp. In either direction the beach just disappears into hazy distances, measured-off by a receding perspective of wooden groins. The only fixed

points are the handful of bungalows on their raised bank and the eponymous creek running out across the beach into the waves.

Skegness is in retreat from the tideline, a flickering jukebox of a town on the corner of that great square indentation into the east coast– The Wash. Here the demarcation between sea and land blurs in mudflats and sandbanks, a receptacle for the outfall of rivers flowing from middle England: the Witham at Boston, the Welland at Fosdyke, the Nene at Sutton Bridge and, finally, the Great Ouse at Kings Lynn where the simply stunning seventeenth-century Customs House looks out over the spruced-up quays.

above
Hunstanton's layer
cake cliffs of chalk and
'gingerbread' carstone

top
Local beer mat (c. 1960)

right
Blakeney Quay, Norfolk

Hunstanton to Lowestoft

Now we're in Norfolk, with Hunstanton facing west over The Wash. Many years ago I disturbingly saw the illuminated big wheel at Skegness on the horizon from here. The coastline turns to face north and becomes a long beautiful stretch of salt marshes and sea roads running down to the shore from brick and flint villages, black-tarred huts among gurgling reed-bound creeks, inland horizons marked with dark pines. Thornham, Titchwell, Brancaster Staithe. The glorious crescent of Holkham Bay with its dunes ideal for picnics, Wells-next-the-Sea with holiday-coloured beach huts on stilts. Blakeney swifts racing round quayside chimneys, mysterious Cley-next-the Sea like a tiny lost town from an Eleanor Farjeon story. White smoke appearing like drifting clouds against the blue as a black engine pulls rattling red carriages through yellow cornfields – the North Norfolk Railway running by the sea to Sheringham. Cromer with its traditional pier that doubles-up as a lifeboat station, the tall church tower looking out over crab sellers and fishing boats launched into the waves by a blue Fordson tractor.

The curve of coast continues its radius, but it becomes bleaker after Cromer as it turns to

look east. Empty shores, lost villages. Bacton with its gas terminal humming like a kitchen boiler, Happisburgh with its now privately-run 100ft lighthouse out in the fields and its churchyard filled with the graves of shipwrecked sailors. Between Sea Palling and Caistor-on-Sea the Norfolk Broads appear so close to the sea as though deposited during a storm. The split personality of Great Yarmouth: harbourman in orange overalls servicing oil rig vessels or blousy, laughing day-tripper with a stud in the nose; Lowestoft dreaming of lost Dogger Bank herrings.

above
Oil rig servicing vessel,
Great Yarmouth

top
Landing the catch at Cley-
next-the-Sea, Norfolk

right
Happisburgh
lighthouse, Norfolk

Southwold to Deptford

Aldeburgh Ambience

top left
Seafront lookout tower

top right
Working foreshore

below
Cast-iron Lifeboat sign

The sandy hinterland of Suffolk, the stuff of M.R. James ghost stories. Remote shores, quiet tidal reaches. Southwold lighthouse sitting in the streets like an oversize garden ornament, lost Dunwich under the waves (listen for the church bells on stormy nights), Sizewell nuclear power station, which everyone tries to imagine isn't really there. And then Aldeburgh: cream, pink, pistachio-coloured houses along the front with white wooden balconies to read the *Telegraph* on. Maggie Hambling's steel scallop shell tribute on the shingle, memorial for Benjamin Britten whose music is the town's soundtrack.

The coast below Aldeburgh starts now to fragment, the frayed-edge corner of England made by bird-haunted estuaries, inlets and those places where the sea has been allowed to be itself. Slaughden disappeared when the River Alde turned from the sea to run parallel to the shore past Orford, finally reaching the ocean at Hollesley Bay. Along this stretch of coast we see examples from three different ages of coastal military defence. The first in Orford with its formidable twelfth-century castle, a Henry II bastion that is one of the most complete keeps in the country. Southwards from Aldeburgh the Martello Towers start, a line of defensive gun emplacements built to counter the threat of Napoleonic invasion. There were once 113 towers, like giant upturned sandcastles, stretching round to Seaford in Sussex. And at Bawdsey, the home of radar, tall masts tower over the pines, concrete bunkers in the sandy rabbit-warrened soil.

Felixstowe and Harwich are the business end of this bulge of England, container and ferry ports at the mouths of the Orwell and Stour rivers. Crabknowe Spit, Pye Sand, Pewit Island. The gentile snobbery of Frinton-on-Sea, neatly-edged lawns and private hedges at a respectful distance from breezy Clacton-on-Sea

above left
Restored sail lofts at Tollesbury, Essex

above right
Thames barge *Greta* at Faversham, Kent

with a funfair on the pier. Maybe we will catch glimpses now of brown-sailed Thames barges, the glorious survivors of the workhorse boats that plied the eastern coasts with cargoes of just about anything that would pay their way. They continually race them out of Brightlingsea and other forgotten Essex ports, a reminder of a vanished age of tarred wooden planking, leeboards held on their iron winches, halyards and batten studs, stiff canvas and stiff winds. The staple of Tollesbury and its wooden sail lofts.

Our coastal run of England's eastern seaboard now becomes more estuarine, still the sea but with a character that increasingly reflects the approach of London. Maunsell forts rising high in the air like Wellsian Martians on their spindly legs above the sea off Whitstable (weatherboarding, oysters), iron doors banging in the wind. More obsolete military strategies at the land forts of Coalhouse, Tilbury. Canvey Island (English delta blues from Dr Feelgood) and its grotesque oil refineries countering the Cooling Marshes of Dickens's *Great Expectations* on the opposing shore. Gravesend desperately wanting to be Georgian or even Victorian again and have paddle steamers from Tower Bridge pulling in under the clock tower on the pier; Greenwich and Deptford leaving us in no doubt that London has finally been reached.

Blackpool, Lancashire

Ilfracombe, Devon

Bunny Hotel

Dover, Kent

Sidmouth, Devon

Clacton-on-Sea, Essex

's End, Cornwall

East Runton, Norfolk

y Bay on Sea

East Wittering, West Sussex

e, East Sussex

Blackpool, Lancashire

North Foreland to Eastbourne

The North Foreland lighthouse in Kent marks the start of England's south coast, a bend in the road between Margate and Broadstairs. Then follows Ramsgate (Dunkirk connector), Sandwich (northernmost Cinque Port), Deal (time ball, treacherous Goodwin Sands), Dover (big castle with wartime Hellfire Corner tunnels in the cliffs) and Folkestone, where I first saw a Morris Mini Minor in 1959. That was when I was on holiday in Hythe (church crypt full of skulls) and discovered the Romney, Hythe and Dymchurch Railway that runs out to the lighthouses on the hot shingle of the Dungeness Peninsular, which drifts seawards away from the Romney and Walland Marshes.

Rye and Winchelsea sit on their respective hills: Rye a jumble of cobbled lanes and cobbled tourists, Winchelsea quieter and smarter with its grid pattern of select streets for retired light entertainers and brain surgeons. Old Hastings with tall black-tarred wooden net-drying sheds and a cliff railway, new Hastings with blocks of flats like liners. Bexhill sporting the jazzy De La Warr Pavilion, Eastbourne a Eugenious Birch pier with lion head lamp posts and a very worrying anamatronic clown who does a faultless trapeze act over the amusement arcades.

Beachy Head to Durdle Door

The awe-inspiring Sussex cliffs start their progression westwards; dry South Down valleys cut off vertically, their profiles caught in a switchback rise and fall of chalk. Beachy Head with its lighthouse way down on the inaccessible beach, the extinguished Belle Tout light moved back at great expense from the cliff edge. Birling Gap where the sea threatens to overwhelm the row of coastguard cottages before the last of the Seven Sisters descends to Seaford and Newhaven with its Palmerston fort and booming Dieppe ferries. The unsympathetic scar of Peacehaven's bungalows, built after the First World War and nearly called Anzac-on-Sea, Saltdean with its lido opened in 1938 by Johnny 'Tarzan' Weissmuller, and Rottingdean with its girls' school in superior isolation before the terraces, squares and crescents of Regency Brighton and Hove parade down the seafront.

Worthing and Bognor give way to Selsey Bill, East Wittering and the deep inlets and tides of the Solent, which give Portsmouth and Gosport naval anchorages, Southampton berthing docks for ocean liners and for everyone else somewhere to keep the yacht. All comings and goings divide here each side of the Isle of Wight

opposite
East Sussex
Beachy Head and
lighthouse

above
Worthing guesthouses

right
Victorian maritime
ironwork. Lift tower on
Madiera Drive, Brighton

(Hampshire in microcosm; the island railway running old London Underground stock out on to Ryde Pier) until another rash of development pushes into Dorset, the traffic-jammed roads and streets of Christchurch, Bournemouth, Poole, Swanage, and then a sigh of relief as the coast becomes Dorset proper. I love the names along this solitary and inhospitable coast: St Adhelm's Head, Kimmeridge Ledges, Worbarrow Tout and Durdle Door. Names redolent of deep blue summer days on cliff tops and the almost imperceptible dull boom of waves far below, the occasional cry of a lone seagull gliding in still air.

Weymouth to Burgh Island

A turn southwards for George III's Weymouth, with his colourful statue on the prom and an equally colourful Punch and Judy on the sands. The unsettling hump of limestone hanging by a narrow thread to Weymouth is the Isle of Portland (q.v.), and then the equally odd Chesil Beach running up to Abbotsbury, dividing the sea from the freshwater lakes known to readers of James Meade Faulkner's *Moonfleet*. This is the start of Lyme Bay, the shoreline sweeping round to the Devon border at Lyme Regis with its medieval Cobb, the stone breakwater that curves into the plots of Jane Austen's *Emma* and John Fowles's *The French Lieutenant's Woman*.

The strange unreal world of the Undercliff with its fossilled landslips connects Lyme with Seaton and Beer; Sidmouth faces the shore with Gothic villas decorated by delicate wrought iron and coloured glass. The almost fictional-sounding Budleigh Salterton is followed by Exmouth and, over the Exe Estuary, we are on the Great Western Railway as it hugs the coast around Dawlish – poster land again –, where green GWR locomotives pulled their chocolate and cream coaches through tunnels and cuttings carved out of the deep pink Devon sandstone before turning inland again at

above
Early morning set-up for Punch and Judy at Weymouth, Dorset

right
Mooring buoys by The Cobb, Lyme Regis, Dorset

Teignmouth. Another line of towns now all join up to form Torbay: Torquay, Paignton, Brixham. 'The English Rivière' the travel agents call it.

Dartmouth hides behind its castle, a tug yanking the car ferry over the Dart with ropes from Kingswear where those GWR trains still steam into a station with the obligatory gulls screaming overhead. The soft pastures of the South Hams keeping Dartmoor from the sea. More evocative names: Start Point, Prawle Point, Bolt Tail. Burgh Island with its Pilchard Inn and white Art Deco hotel to suit *Poirot*, a sea tractor to take you there when the tide's in.

left
Railway and sea, Dawlish, Devon

top left
The classic Devon souvenir

above
Burgh Island sea tractor

Plymouth to Bristol

Brunel's masterful Royal Albert Bridge connects Plymouth (gin made with Dartmoor water) with Saltash, Devon with Cornwall and picture postcard harbours at Looe, Fowey, Mevagissey. Henry VIII cloverleaf castles at St Mawes and Pendennis guarding the entrance to the Carrick Roads and Falmouth. The hidden heron-haunted inlets with overhanging trees, Daphne Du Maurier's

Frenchman's Creek with its trace of tobacco on the air. The Manacles, Black Head, Hot Point (yes, really) and foghorns blaring out from the Lizard. Everything gathering to the end of England. Penzance: end of the railway line from Paddington, Land's End: end of the A30 from Hounslow.

The north coast of Cornwall is wilder, less cosseted. Sea mists blow in across the Penwith Peninsular, shrouding Lanyon Quoit, Men-a-Tol. Pale creamy light diffuses St Ives, taking the edge off granite cottages and letting down the starkness of the Tate Gallery's Cornish outpost. St Agnes, Perranporth. Newquay with its Huer's House, where they watched out for the red stain of pilchards in the sea. Now it's the stain of flourescent swimwear sliding about on the waves. Trevose Head, the Camel Estuary with Rick Stein land one side and Betjeman's Trebetherick on the other. Doom Bar on the Camel Outfall and on the beer labels, beaches around Rock obscured in summer by Boden t-shirts.

Doc Martin's Port Isaac still works for me, boats leaning on the beach, fresh fish for sale in a wet-floored shop. Deserted Port Quin, surviving and reviving Boscastle, Hawker's Morwenstow with his little clifftop hut for

Anchor before turning inland at Watchet with its bright red soldier of a lighthouse on the little working quay. The Quantock Hills end on the shore between West Quantoxhead and Kilve before the coast turns northwards by Burnham-on-Sea with its enigmatic wooden lighthouse on the beach acting as a turning point for sand yachts racing down from Berrow. This is now the Bristol Channel, with Weston-super-Mare donkeys and Clevedon's filigree pier on its shores, before it becomes the Severn Estuary closing in to Bristol.

opposite bottom
Huer's House, Newquay

opposite top
A load of scallops from the Captain

above
House on the quayside, Boscastle, Cornwall

contemplating the souls of drowned sailors and then we're back in Devon. Appledore, Bideford, Ifracombe and Combe Martin where Exmoor starts to meet the sea. Lynton and Lynmouth, twin sufferers in the flood tragedy of August 1952. Countisbury Head and its hidden squat lighthouse clinging to the cliff, Porlock Bay and Minehead. From here West Somerset Railway trains run by the sea past Dunster and Blue

right
Andrew Martin's evocative detective novel set in Edwardian Blackpool

far right
Fleetwood bowling green and one of two Decimus Burton lighthouses

New Brighton to Maryport

The English coast starts again on the Wirral with the bleeping gaming machines of New Brighton; Fort Perch and its rusting lighthouse watching over the Crosby Channel where the Irish and Isle of Man ferries enter and leave the Mersey. Liverpool is worth a detour to see not only the impressive bulk of the Albert Docks but also the Pier Head buildings, like a miniature waterside New York. Formby sand dunes featuring in Beryl Bainbridge's *A Quiet Life*, Southport featuring Pleasureland and a lawnmower museum, before the Ribble Estuary separates it from posh Lytham St Anne's. Blossoming trees in red-brick terraced streets, men in Panamas taking small dogs for walks on the wide greensward by a Fylde windmill, women going to the hairdressers in expensive convertibles. Everyone trying to ignore the noisy neighbour, Blackpool. Golden Mile, an Eiffel Tower with a ballroom and organ, Ken Dodd, real trams that hum all the way up to the quieter pleasures of Fleetwood with Decimus Burton lighthouses and bowling greens in evening sunlight. Lonely enchanting shores by Cockersand Abbey and the Lune Estuary, Morecambe with Eric's statue and the Midland Hotel that once had murals by another Eric – Ravilious – and his best friend Edward Bawden.

    With an expert guide you can cross

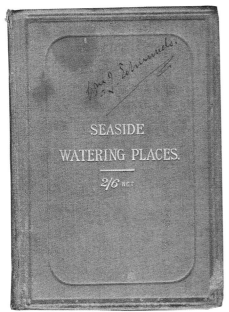

above left
The essential seaside guide. This particular edition for the 1902/03 season

above right
Almost the last of England: Maryport, Cumbria

Morecambe Bay at low tide; in earlier times they even took coaches across to avoid the detour through Carnforth. Grange-over-Sands railway station is practically on the beach, Ulverston has a faux lighthouse in memory of a secretary to the Admiralty, Barrow-in-Furness builds Trident submarines. The coastline now edges its way round the Lake District, a railway running right next to the shore from Millom to St Bees, with a station just for the nuclear reprocessors at Sellafield. Tiny Ravenglass, Saltcoats, Seascale with its sandstone locomotive water tower and St Bees with its rotund lighthouse on top of 300ft high cliffs, the last coal-fired light in Britain. Remains of industry haunt Whitehaven and Workington, where coal seams ran for miles under the sea, and at Maryport where, in the nineteenth century, ships were loaded with railway lines hammered out in Cumberland and sent all over the world. A little cast-iron lighthouse on a cinder road winding to the pier and the pounding Solway Firth finally marks the end of our brief tour of England by the sea.

SHOPKEEPERS' SHOPS

SHOP EARLY

opposite
Butcher's greaseproof wrapping paper for Homewood's shop in Biddenden, Kent. Note the telephone number

This book isn't in the business of knocking the French, after all we English love a nice runny camembert, fortifying clarets and Citroëns like the one in *Maigret*. It's just that they have some odd ways of insulting us. I once accidentally drove my car into the middle of a period film location in the Cévennes while the camera was turning and got surrounded by cross technicians in *travail bleu* waving pliers at me. They took one look at my number plate and started shouting 'Rost Bif! Rost Bif!'. Imagine a Frenchman making the same mistake in Sussex and the crew shouting, 'Choux Pastry! Choux Pastry!'. I say all this because the best Napoleon could come up with before getting a seeing-to at Trafalgar and Waterloo was that we were a 'nation of shopkeepers', as if his own country wasn't full of *pâtisseries*, *boulangeries* and *boucheries*.

Yes we had shops, and we were proud of them. Ever since the medieval market stall selling offal and turnips went indoors and let down the shutters to act as a counter we have had shops to go into and buy things. Everything we had a need for, which meant that once we'd got beyond just wanting 'rost bif' and fruit and veg, our hearts' desires could be found on the high street. Have a look at a photograph taken of a village or town main street on a hot sunny day in the first half of the twentieth century and the first things one notices are the sunblinds. Each one denoting the presence of an individual shop. 'Individual' being the operative word, for these were the premises of local traders, the shopkeepers everyone knew and trusted and who, on a day like the one in the photograph, would probably stand in their doorways remarking on the good weather to passers-by.

Not So Super Markets

There is no doubt that the biggest change to our shopping habits has been brought about by supermarkets. An American import in the 1950s, they were originally 'self-service' discount stores that introduced us to the tactile pleasures of the wire basket. They have evolved now into the new religion, occupying the epicentre of daily lives once taken up with listening to the wireless and reading bits out of the Bible. Turkey Twizzlers are sold next to pairs of spectacles; car insurance next to pairs of kippers. Most supermarkets dictate the size and shape of fruit to *über* growers who defoliate the countryside with polytunnels so we can eat strawberries in January, and make dairy farmers grovel for the few coins paid for their milk. And they do it all with clever little catchphrases to hide the fact that they have destroyed more local businesses than the Blitz. But at least they're usually stuck out of town next to other dismal mass retailers in a horrible *mélange* of bark chippings and cheap petrol stations. Of course they realise they can still make some money on the high street so have spawned micro-versions of themselves, contributing to the dire overall effect of streetscapes reduced visually to lines of plastic identikit signage with no regard for the integrity of the buildings they're foisted on.

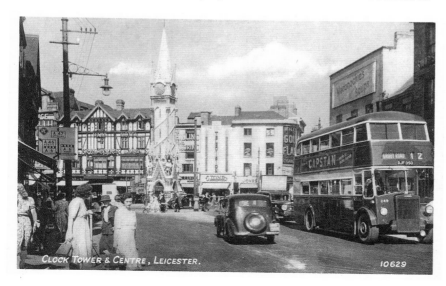

CLOCK TOWER & CENTRE, LEICESTER.   10629

Unchained Stores

But there was a time, not so long ago, when even a chain store somehow fitted in. Not through any considered plan, more from an unconscious desire to simply do the right thing. In 1978 I photographed many shops in Ludlow, a quintessentially English market town in Shropshire. It was in the run-up to Christmas and the market hall was filled with the foggy breath of townsfolk haggling over boughs of holly and mistletoe. Fruiterers laid out round-ended boxes of dates on their window sills and big sweet jars were paraded behind a window that had 'Cadburys' stuck on the glass in thin white metal letters. But there was also a Boots the Chemist and a Woolworths. Boots have always tried to do the right thing by the high street (one of their original signs is still on the corner of a Canterbury street exactly as it appears in the film *A Canterbury Tale* (q.v.) made in 1944) and

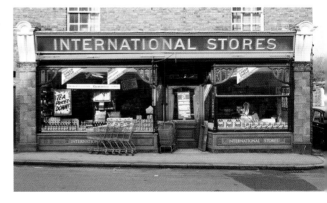

here in Ludlow they used a gilded wooden cut-out version of their exuberant signature logo on the half-timbered building. Even the Woolies fitted in, with its dark wood doors with brass kick plates, although I noticed inside that a stack of wire baskets was presaging things to come, just as the ubiquitous trolleys did when I photographed the tiled and gilded fascia of the International Stores in Uppingham in the same year.

Grocers and Butchers

Even in 1978 Ludlow was an anchronism, possibly because none of the major supermarket players were in town. Ludlow had managed to stave off any unwelcome incursions, but finally Tesco elbowed their way in and change was inevitable. But the town has survived, perhaps owing something to Michelin-starred cooks moving in with their aubergine fritters, but certainly to the Food and Drink Festival which does so much to promote good local food from good local shopkeepers. One of the highlights is the Sausage Trail that involves Ludlow's *five* independent butchers, a heart-warming indication that supermarkets don't have it all their own way. Butchers have survived better than most other traditional shops and, with the entreaties of proper cooks like Hugh Fearnley Whittingstall and Rick Stein making us appreciate again the connection between the beasts in the fields and the meat on our

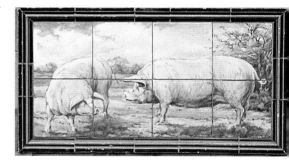

plates, they will hopefully continue to prosper.

Grocery shops have not faired as well, after all food is the staple of the big boys. Reduced now to a few tins in the village shop (if we're lucky to still have one) those with any presence are those that have metamorphosed into up-market food emporia. There is a superb example in Penrith where Graham's have retained the original signage, the 'Family Grocers' legend sharing space on the sign with 'Agricultural Seed Cake and Manure Merchants'.

June			July		
27	4.6 J Beef	5 1½	18	14 Veal C	1 7½
July 1	16 Rf otts	1 7s	do	2.5 Bt necke	2 4
	13 Veal C	1 0.2	22	4.15 Loin Vl	4 11½
	8½ e sirloin	8 9		16 Rf otte	1 7s
4	2.10 Bt necke	2 7½			
5	13 Rf otts	11½			10 0½
6	1.2 Veal C	1 5	Paid July 29. 11		
8	5½ rits Bf	5 0½	almts		
			Chitty Hodges & Higgs		
Paid July 15.11 £ 1.6.7					
almts			27	15 Veal C	1 2½
Chitty Hodges & Higgs			29	4.c O Beef	3 11
				1.2 Rf otte	1 4
11	1.3 Veal C	1 6.			
12	1.10 Rf otte	1 11			6 5½
15	3.7 Bt necke	3 5½	Paid Aug 5. 11		
P'd July 22.11			almts		
Chitty Hodges & Higgs 6.10½			Chitty Hodges & Higgs		

It is respectfully requested that this book may be sent in on or before Saturday, as we make up our accounts every Monday & redeliver the book to you on the Tuesday.

Smith's, Billesdon

opposite

How to buy fruit: a brown paper bag and a short, pithy exhortation to do it all again

above and right

Last remnants of a busy shop life: Smith's in Billesdon, Leicestershire

I was lucky enough to photograph the interior of a village shop in Billesdon, Leicestershire a short while before it finally closed in the late 1970s. The original shopfittings had never been altered, and I was confronted by the extraordinary spectacle of past merchandise such as big empty tea canisters alongside Tallon ballpens (slogan: 'more writing-miles per Tallon') and cards of 7 O'Clock razor blades. The shelves were still edged with tin advertisement strips for Brand's Sauce and Colman's DSF Mustard. Carter's Tested Seeds dispensers, long empty of seed packets, held curling black and white postcards of the village. The shop owner, incidentally one of the first women pilots, opened a thick cardboard box and showed me a perfect unworn boy's tweed suit still wrapped in tissue paper. It looked like something out of *The Go-Between* (q.v.), certainly it was Edwardian. The lady's father rented the shop from the Co-op and specialised in providing the local ladies of fashion with silk and corsets that he brought up from Harrods. There's another film there.

74

Cundell's, Dartmouth, Devon

Beaman's, Audlem, Cheshire

Shoe Repairers, Totnes, Devon

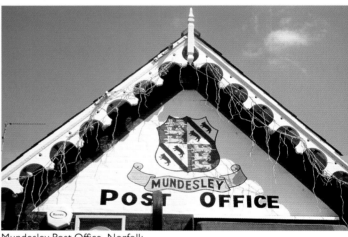

Mundesley Post Office, Norfolk

South Brink Farm Shop, Wisbech, Cambridgeshire

Wadenhoe Post Office, Northamptonshire

...ngham, Rutland

Hall's Bookshop, Tunbridge Wells, Kent

...ombe Fishmongers, Devon

Freeman's, Ramsey, Cambridgeshire

...n's Cycle Shop, Ashby-de-la-Zouch, Leicestershire

Pillar's, Dartmouth, Devon

Post Offices

above
General Post Office cipher

below left
Rampisham Post Office, Dorset

below centre
Kirkby Stephen Post Office, Cumbria

below right
Weekley Post Office, Northamptonshire

Village shops will often double up as the post office, a secure little enclave tucked away at the back by the firelighters and Winalot. Hundreds have now closed, more are under threat of closure over the demands to computerise, which to many of the souls running them must be akin to asking them to train for a moon landing. The post office is a vital village resource, along with regular buses, but sadly rural affairs are not a priority with politicians far more concerned with banning country pursuits like smoking in pubs. The post office took on the role of village office with pens on strings and much blotting paper, the post mistress leaving her counter now and then to connect a local telephone call on a switchboard sprouting plugs and leads. We never thought it odd that the GPO looked after both the post and the telephones and we're glad that the link still clings on, the rural scene enlivened by post boxes and telephones both painted 'pillar box' red.

How much longer will we be able to enjoy sticking a stamp on an envelope in the dim recesses of a thatched Rampisham, smell the roses round the door of a Kirkby Stephen or a Weekley? How soon before we simply don't need them anymore because the Royal Mail has been out-sourced to Burkina Faso, the rhythmic thump of a rubber stamp a distant folk memory?

right
Aldwincle Post Office and
Stores, Northamptonshire

far right top
Sign in Docking, Norfolk

far right bottom
Sentinels outside
Clitheroe Post Office,
Lancashire

Ryme Intrinsica, Dorset

Felsted, Essex

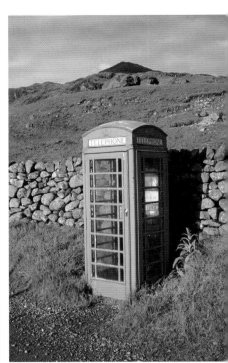

Hardknott Pass, Cumbria

Godalming, Surrey

Seething, Norfolk

Barrowden, Rutland

sham, Kent

Sudborough, Northamptonshire

Fingest, Buckinghamshire

sby, Leicestershire

Great Malvern, Worchestershire

Buckworth, Cambridgeshire

top right
Yes please, live *or* cooked.
Sign outside the Port Isaac
Fish Shop, Cornwall

bottom right
Dungeness, Kent

opposite
The world famous
Aldeburgh Fish and Chip
Shop in Suffolk, minus the
queue down the street

Fish and Fish 'n' Chips

However, our collective folk memories never
let us forget that we are surrounded by lots of
sea with fish swimming about in it. Fish which,
it sometimes appears, can be pulled out of the
ocean with equanimity by every country in
Europe, even those without a coastline. Except
us. The trawler fleets diminish but we can still
buy fresh fish directly from fishermen; even in
deepest Northamptonshire we have a man who
comes from the Norfolk coast with oysters.
Nearer to the sea Port Isaac in Cornwall has a
wonderfully fishy shop right next to where the
crab and lobster boats lie at anchor, leaning
precipitously to one side when the tide runs
out. Aldeburgh in Suffolk (q.v.) has a couple of
tarred sheds on the shingle selling the catch
amongst rusty winches and wire hausers, and
just down the road the Pinney family still
smoke their daily landings, flavouring the air
above the red-brick chimneys of Orford.

There are around 8,600 fish and chip shops
in the UK, but back in Aldeburgh there is one
with few equals. Margaret Thompson has been
frying fish here for thirty years, never putting
flour in her batter and only using pure
vegetable oil. No beef dripping here. Regularly
appearing in the style charts of weekend papers
the red-brick building is marked out in the early
evening by a queue stretching down the street
towards Slaughden. Eventually they shuffle
inside, watching and listening to the sudden
hiss of fish immersing into the fryers, the tap-
tap of wire baskets of chips about to be tossed
out. 'Salt? Vinegar?'.

Shoe Shops

The traditional shoe shop is getting as rare as traditional shoes. Not all of us want to slope about in over-white trainers that always look three sizes too big, and when we buy shoes we don't want a 'retailing experience'. Ideally we just want stacks of shoe boxes reached by a portable ladder, a few comfy chairs and one of those sloping rubber-matted foot rests. We'll know want we want and as far as fitting goes we'd like to be able to shove our feet into an X-ray machine that turns our feet skeletal and green inside our boots. If you want to know what that was about watch *Billion Dollar Brain*, where Michael Caine puts a Thermos flask in one on his way to the airport and discovers very suspicious-looking eggs in it.

But if you want a real shoe shop you should try a pair on in Tricker's London shop in Jermyn Street. These are shoes that have been made in Northampton since 1829, shoes where the words 'bespoke' and 'handmade' are as liberally applied as polish on a pair of brogues. Not many pairs are on display, most lurk inside wooden cupboards, and they're the kind of shoes that if you wreck them (hard to do) Tricker's will rebuild them like you would an Aston Martin. Northamptonshire was once full of shoemakers: red-brick factories looking out over every street of the towns stretching down the Nene Valley, industrious communities of clickers and welters, outworkers toiling in their 'barns' in back gardens, soles and heels amongst the sweet peas.

Chemists

above left
Dwelly's Chemists,
Chatteris, Cambridgeshire
(c. 1980)

above right
Kodak Verichrome 120
film box

bottom right
Razor blades 'tested
and packed' by the
Dread-Nowt Co. in Hull.
The name comes from
the HMS *Dreadnought*
launched in 1906. The
reverse of the packet says:
'It's 'coom' at last. It's
f'ra Yorkshire. By gum
lads– it's a good 'un' '

I was brought up in and out of chemists' shops. My father worked in Boots dispensaries for nearly fifty years, so we were used to a world of strange liquids and powders. Occasionally he would do a trick for us where he put tap water into a glass, poured it into another one and it turned red. On holiday we had to visit other Boots shops where he would introduce himself to the manager while we shuffled our feet in embarrassment. But they all made a lasting impression. The immaculately made-up shop girls advising on both face powder and photographic films, the rows of obsolete carbuoys and gold-labelled jars still kept on the higher shelves, and the products we only ever saw in the chemist or in our grandmothers' cupboards: Fynnon Salts, Energen Rolls, Dread-Nowt Razor Blades.

There was always a bentwood chair for customers waiting for their 'scrip' to arrive in cardboard pill boxes or corked glass bottles, perhaps a life-size cut-out of a Kodak girl in a striped swimsuit, often a glass cabinet with mysterious grey packets marked Durex Gossamer. I'd seen this on a mirror in the barbers and my father was very unforthcoming when asked about it. He talked more about farmers coming in to be fitted with something called a 'truss' and always wore his old white dispensary coats to work on his Ford Popular.

THE REGULATOR, with Patent Drip Protector.

Hardware

Now here's a good idea. We frequently need things like screws, nails, lengths of wood, turpentine, balls of string, coal scuttles, galvanised dustbins, fireguards, garden trugs and paraffin for the Aladdin greenhouse heater. So what we need is a place where we can get all these things without having to ask a clueless youth in a warehouse. There would be a shopkeeper in a khaki overall with a Biro in the pocket, and he (or she) would know everything and offer friendly advice. Behind this shopkeeper would be ranks of wooden drawers going up to the ceiling with labels on each one saying things like 'Countersunk ¾ wood'. We'd get exactly the number of door catches we wanted and if we popped back in half an hour our wood would be cut to length. It would all be called an 'ironmonger'.

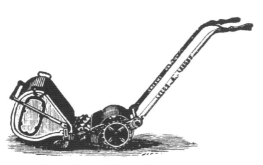

Single-Handed Lawn Mower.

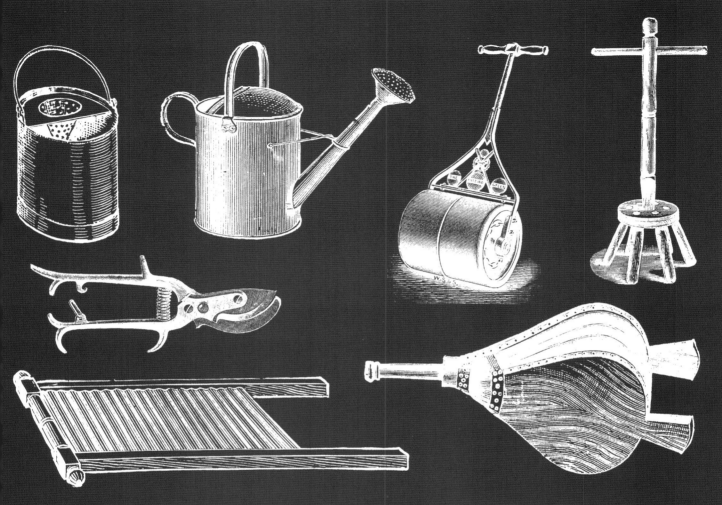
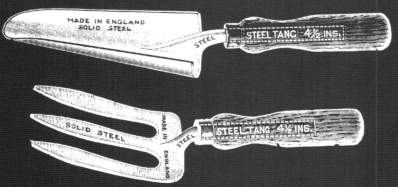
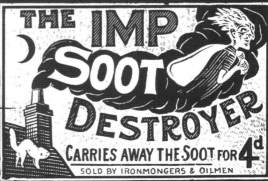

COLOURED COUNTIES

Here of a Sunday morning
My love and I would lie,
And see the coloured counties,
And hear the larks so high
About us in the sky

'A Shropshire Lad', A.E. Housman

opposite
Detail of the England map
from *Collins British Isles
and World Atlas*– 'A school
atlas for the air age'
(c. 1960)

When I first read Housman's words I immediately thought of my school atlas and its
partitioning of England's counties in different
colours. Only later did I come to realise what a
perfect description 'coloured counties' was for
the richly-patterned fields and woods of
England. The words came back to me a few
years ago when I stood on top of Beacon Hill
south of Newbury on a beautiful August
evening. Red combine harvesters were crawling
across the brilliantly yellow Hampshire fields
with clouds of dust blurring their progress, blue
tractors ploughed fields already divested of
their wheat and barley, turning the land back to
deep brown corduroy. Green pastures were
spotted with Freisians like a butter poster and a
row of red-brick cottages with grey tiled roofs
marked a road winding across to Burghclere.
This immense patchwork was stitched together
with hedges, copses and woodland reduced to
the same almost black-green by the westering
light, all of it fading into a purple distance

announced by the wooded arc of Cottington's
Hill. Highclere Castle was a blue cube below
me to the northwest with a St George's flag on
a turret blowing smartly in the breeze and to
the west, as the sun started to lose its brassy
heat, the woods around hidden Faccombe and
Linkenholt became pale and backlit. The
south towards Winchester, Southampton and
the sea became a dusty darkening haze, and as
I walked slowly back down the white chalk
track that cut through the slope of the hill I
marvelled that what I had seen was in fact only
a handful of square miles, a thumbnail sketch
of just one of England's coloured counties.

caster

Y O R K

W. Riding York E. Riding

Burnley **Bradford** **Hull**

Leeds

Halifax

S Doncaster Grimsby

ter Oldham Huddersfield Lindsey

Warrington Stockport Lincoln

HIRE Macclesfield NOTTS **LINCOLN**

DERBY **Nottingham** Boston

Stoke Kest. Cromer

Stafford Derby Holl. Kings Lynn

ry STAFFS. Grantham **NORFOLK**

Leicester RUT. Soke Wisbech D Gt.

E N G LEICS. L A N Norwich Yarn

hampton **BIRMINGHAM** Peterborough Ely

ster **Coventry** HUNTS West East

WARWICK Rugby Northampton **SUFFOLK**

WORCS Warwick Bedford Cambridge Ipswich

RD Worcester BEDS. Colchester Harwich

reford Buckingham ESSEX

Cheltenham Aylesbury HERTS. Hertford Chelmsford

GLOUCS. OXFORD BUCKS LONDON

Gloucester Oxford MIDDX.

Swindon BERKS Windsor Croydon Chatham

Bristol Reading KENT Canterbury

th WILTS Aldershot SURREY Maidstone

Leicestershire and Neighbours

I suppose my 'heart country' is an area comprising the eastern uplands of Leicestershire with northeastern Northamptonshire and Rutland, the smallest county of them all. This is still largely unknown England, a landscape of sheep pastures and arable fields divided by the hawthorn hedges and spinneys beloved of foxhunters. Many of the lanes were once wide-verged drovers' roads, now heavy with cow parsley in late spring, both linking and avoiding the settlements on either side in equal measure. In High Leicestershire you will find quiet villages and farms of orange brick with blue slate roofs, the colours changing abruptly as the land rises up onto the limestone belt. Here the buildings turn to stone, each village reflecting the underlying geology: gingerbread-coloured ironstone with little pieces of ore stuck in it

like currants, silver limestone that sometimes appears as a brilliant white in strong morning sunlight, sheep-grey in afternoon rain. Fine ashlar-faced churches rise behind ancient yews; modest halls and granges are found at the end of avenues of limes.

This is still a working agricultural landscape, despite the grey paperwork of DEFRA and their political masters in Belgium. The country towns – Melton Mowbray, Market Harborough, Oakham, Uppingham – still serve great swathes of this undulating countryside, which remains virtually untouched since the Enclosure Acts. True, there has been the inevitable grubbing-up of ancient hedgerows to make larger fields, but signposts at lonely crossroads still point to secret hidden places– Launde Abbey, Withcote Hall, Oxey Farm. And the maps still declaim man's imprint on the land: Botany Bay Fox Covert, America Lodge, the earthwork-like Robin-a-Tiptoe Hill, only 221ft high and named after a

top left
Open landscape near
Noseley, Leicestershire

top right
Knob Hill Farm,
Horninghold,
Leicestershire

right
Winning Foot Hill, a
drovers' road crossing
the Lyveden Valley in
Northamptonshire

local whose toes touched the ground when he was strung up from a gallows on its windy ridge. Lost villages traced in summer evening shadow lines in the fields: Noseley, Othorpe, Ingarsby, Cold Newton. Lost highways keeping faith now only with the badger and fox: the wind in the long grasses of the Sewstern Lane up near the Lincolnshire border, the empty Gartree Road cutting across it all in an unerring line that separates the villages on each side of it– Cranoe, Glooston, Slawston and the evocatively-named Carlton Curlieu. Forgotten drovers' roads disappearing and reappearing in the fields, watched over now by mad hares and little owls in isolated oaks. A landscape that keeps a low profile with no pretensions, no airs or graces; a landscape that is intensely English.

Much in Little

above left
Rutland boundary
sign near Stockerston,
Leicestershire

above right
Parkland railings in
Ayston, Rutland

H.E. Bates called Rutland '... the dillin pig of
the litter' but admitted it was perhaps the best
of all the East Midland counties. Certainly it is
the smallest, unceremoniously grabbed by
Leicestershire in 1974 but returned to its
rightful place on the map in 1995. It sits between
Leicestershire to the west, Lincolnshire both
to the north and east, and to the south
Northamptonshire with the River Welland as
the border. The Great North Road thunders
through between Stamford and Grantham,
leaving an odd hinterland to the east that is
more Lincolnshire in character. But for the
most part stone-built villages gather round the
two towns of Oakham and Uppingham, both
with large public schools. If you have to choose
between the two, always head for Uppingham,
a little hilltop town full of ironmongers, bookshops and an art gallery where Piper lithographs
rub shoulders with Kandinsky woodcuts.

Nobody came to Rutland much, except
dignatories leaving giant horseshoes in
Oakham Castle or Göring and von Ribbentrop
in the 1930s driving around in a local Chrysler
taxi to go hunting and play golf. But a bucolic
blitzkreig ensued in the mid-70s when the River
Gwash was dammed above Empingham,
forming one of the largest man-made sheets of

water in Europe. Villages disappeared, the baroque church of St Matthew at Normanton very nearly drowned but instead reduced to a half-submerged curiosity, stripped of its church-yard yews and railings. Now everyone sails, cycles and walks past it, just an intriguing landmark to photograph on a day out at Rutland Water.

Rutland is much more than this. Turn off onto the by-roads and find the remarkable, beautiful churches: Exton with a towering Grinling Gibbons monument, Brooke hiding an Elizabethan interior and Stoke Dry a secret room above the porch. Gaunt windmill shells alone in the fields (South Luffenham, Ketton); a Voysey house (North Luffenham) and; one of my favourite hidden places, less than a mile from the south shore of the water, the agricultural buildings at Normanton Lodge Farm. And every-where the limestone cottages, often thatched, many retaining the heavy Collyweston slates on the roofs which aren't slates at all but local stone that in extreme cold splits into tile thickness.

left
Lyddington, Rutland

above
Normanton Lodge Farm
buildings, Rutland

Norfolk

Travelling east from Rutland the A47 descends from the limestone belt at Peterborough on to the billiard table fens that stretch out to the western edges of Norfolk. This is the road that strikes straight across the county to Norwich, and any diversion off to the right or left will

quickly get the traveller lost in a maze of country lanes leading to isolated villages and forgotten towns. Noël Coward is always quoted as saying, 'Very flat, Norfolk', so obviously never got further than Downham Market, though it's true the county doesn't have many viewpoints unless you're standing on a cliff edge or on top of a water tower. But there is a perceptible rise and fall of contours that hide remote villages in a green and yellow agricultural landscape where only the grey flint church towers give them away. Norfolk flint and chalk, the last ripples of a seismic shift that formed Dorset downs and Chiltern ridges, finally weakening in the last run up to the North Sea.

Churches are the thing in the East Anglian landscape, around 650 built before 1700 in Norfolk alone. There are numerous round towers, which antiquarians tell us were easier to build than square ones. Not really. A round tower is more than likely just a style preference. Many churches are empty ruins out in the fields echoing to the jack-jack staccatos of daws, but still as essentially Norfolk as brick cottages augmented with pebbles or flints and the country estates behind poacher-inviting walls and dark pines. Deep red Melton Constable Hall (q.v.) with its cucumber forcing houses and game larders, immaculate Raynham surrounded by shrubs and yellow gravel sweeps looking out over wide cornfields near Fakenham. Thomas Coke's pale brick Holkham in its vast deer park, turning its broad back to the sea, and Jacobean Blickling, the orange brick and Ketton stone showstopper with its lantern turret against the woods.

Suffolk

top right
Doorway, Sudbury

bottom right
Pargetting on Sparrowes
House, Ipswich

Suffolk is divided from Norfolk by the Rivers Waveney and Little Ouse and forms the central portion of East Anglia, a rough parallelogram pinned down at the corners by Mildenhall, Lowestoft, Felixstowe and Haverhill. Compared to Norfolk the landscape is closer knit, a more complex web of lanes joining tiny hamlets and myriad farmsteads amongst the oaks. Oaks that trace their sap-lines back to the trees that gave their wood for the timber frames of the county's buildings. Timber framing is the Suffolk vernacular, infilled with herring-boned brickwork or more usually plaster, painted in a palette of colour that includes the oft-quoted 'Suffolk Pink', once made from mixing pig's blood with limewash. Or so they say. But the walls could equally be saffron yellow, mustard, cream or apricot. (Occasionally someone will miss the point and we will be greeted by the eye-watering sight of deep purple and magenta cottages through the trees.) Often they will be ornamented with pargetting, the art of drawing with a stick in the still-wet plaster; decoration that can range from simple comb effects to flowers, foliage and figures in high relief.

above left
St John Baptist, Snape, Suffolk

above right
Sailing barge *Cygnet* at Snape Wharf

Outside of the villages the countryside is marked out with halls and manor houses, many with deep green moats reflecting the colour wash and tall brick chimneys in their still waters. The showpiece churches tower over their parishes, awe-inspiring expressions of thanksgiving and not a little pride from prosperous medieval wool merchants: Eye, Lavenham, Long Melford, Blythburgh, Kersey. Now and then a flag fluttering over the rooftops betrays the presence of a castle: Framlingham's wildly-impressive curtain walls, the almost original polygonal keep at Orford still watching over the coast from Aldeburgh to Bawdsey.

As we near this shoreline we arrive in a hinterland of heaths and river marshes haunted by the melancholic cry of the curlew, the creak of oars or sudden flap of sail canvas above the reed beds. And everywhere the sense of a vanished agricultural past, every village an *Akenfield*. The legacy of a traction engine works in Leiston still written in the streets of raw brick terraces, the huge rambling maltings at Snape now singing to a different tune.

opposite

Essex vernacular: Black weatherboarding and orange pantiles at Sparrow Hall near Hatfield Broad Oak

above left

Lightship on the Woodrolfe Creeke, Tollesbury, Essex

above right

Post mill at Aythrope Reading, Essex

Essex

Common perceptions of Essex can all too often revolve around its close proximity to London and stereotypes about its population, which would have us believe that only taxi drivers and girls with white shoes live there. In fact this is a large, very rural county, only built-up in the southwest corner around the main roads radiating out from the capital to Harlow, Chelmsford and Southend. Its shredded coast extends from Shoeburyness to Harwich, the estuaries of the Crouch, Blackwater, Colne and Stour reaching far inland, a lonely landscape of atmospheric inlets filled with the eerie sound of mewing seabirds and the ever-present clink-clink of wire tapping the aluminium masts of moored boats. Oysters are harvested and those not sent off to London are levered open in wooden shacks on muddy creeks.

Inland Essex, like Norfolk and Suffolk, reveals itself slowly to those with the time and patience to drive round in circles. This is very easy to do, since in some areas a distinct lack of signposts means a frustrating guessing game. The map's not much help, but at least it gives you a good idea of what to expect with village and hamlet names like Matching Tye and Molehill Green. The local buildings are timber-framed, the houses plastered and usually painted off-white, but mostly the Essex vernacular is expressed in weatherboarding, particularly on the barns where black-tarred timbers contrast so effectively with bright orange roof pantiles. And in between it all the clapboard windmills, a ubiquitous symbol for all of East Anglia.

Outwood, Surrey

Whissendine, Rutland

Stembridge, Somerset

Great Bircham, Norfolk

Wainfleet, Lincolnshire

Ashton, Somerset

ne, Norfolk

Sarre, Kent

Saxtead Green, Suffolk

rd, Lincolnshire

Chesterton, Warwickshire

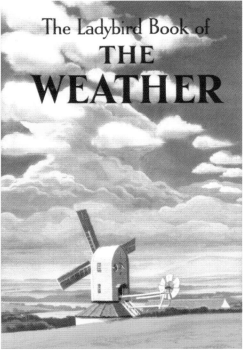

The Ladybird Book of
THE
WEATHER

Cover based on Thorpeness, Suffolk

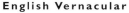

English Vernacular

Stone Belt

A motoring tour through all of these East Anglian counties could easily be accomplished in a day, but each county is markedly different from its neighbour.

It all comes down to the availability of building materials before the canals and railways enabled the transport of stone, bricks, tiles and slates to locations far from their original source. Local craftsmen used what was immediately to hand and followed techniques handed down within a relatively small area, outside influences being the preserve of the rich. (The church always found the money to build in stone wherever they wanted.) So our landscape changes not only because of the topography of hills, rivers, agricultural and commercial development, but also in relation to the lie of the land beneath the surface which determines regional differences and English vernacular styles.

The most obvious example is the limestone belt that starts modestly in West Dorset, thickens out into Gloucestershire and the Cotswolds to run north through Oxfordshire, Northamptonshire and Rutland until it forms the thin Lincolnshire Edge before only just making it into the East Riding above the Humber. 'Limestone' is a generic – the geologists will enthuse about oolites and the Lower Estuarine Series and quarrymen will talk about Ancaster, Barnack Rag, the beautiful creamy Weldon – but to the casual observer it means cottages and houses in a subtly changing variety of stone in a diagonal line across the country. In northeast Northamptonshire you can stand in Duddington, Apethorpe, Bulwick or wander around exquisite country churchyards in Southwick or Wadenhoe and be hard put not to think you're in the Cotswolds.

Fenland

meres and sodden isles peopled only by monks, eel-catchers and wild-eyed fugitives. The buildings stand out here like ships on the horizon: neat brick chapels, gaunt churches, Georgian farmhouses in stands of chestnuts, disused pumping stations with tall chimney stacks alone on the banks of brimming rivers and wide artificial drains. The Fens encompass much that I find fascinating: houses and cottages subsiding drunkenly into the fields as a result of peat wastage, abandoned farm machinery in isolated tarred sheds, giant sluice gates dark against seemingly boundless skies.

To the east of the stone country the great open horizons of the Fens extend out to The Wash across north Cambridgeshire, parts of east Norfolk and south Lincolnshire. A landscape where huge skies compete with endless level vistas of vast fields growing cereals, vegetables and fruit on an industrial scale, a countryside where man's influence is comparatively recent. Not until the seventeenth century were serious attempts made to drain the traditional fenlands, an oozing landscape of reed-bound

top left
Glassmoor Bank pumping station, Cambridgeshire

top right
Fenland fields and drain, Lincolnshire

bottom
At home in the landscape, a 1957 Land Rover

Chalk and Cheese

Downland dominates the South. The Ridgeway, the Chilterns and shallow East Anglian hills, the North and South Downs running eastwards to their dramatic cliff-top finales in Kent and Sussex respectively. The buildings in the coombes and valleys are of a variety of materials: chalk, clunch, brick, cob and the ever present flint. Much of it roofed in that chocolate box favourite, cosy humps of thatch. Between the long fingers of chalk are the Wealden clays and villages of soft red brick, white-painted windows and tilehanging, the late seventeenth-century weatherproofer often only applied to gable ends and upper storeys.

Moving southwest we discover harsh granite rubble in Cornwall, with slate from that enormous hole in the earth's surface at Delabole; monolithic field and farm gateposts like sarsen stones. Everything here is hunkered down against the weather, the passage of narrow lanes marked by stark trees bent to the will of high winds. Devon and Somerset appear warmer, responding to the deep pink soils with a mixture of cob and thatch, and moorland granites perhaps softened with liberal coats of paint. And then of course you go to a place like Langport and everything gets thrown up in the air with just about every material and finish going.

above
Gatepost near Men-a-Tol, Cornwall

top
Tile hanging in Brasted, Kent

top centre
Keeping an eye on the landscape, the White Horse, Uffington, Oxfordshire

top right
Langport, Somerset

Malvern Vistas

above left
Worcestershire from the
Malvern Hills

above right
Herefordshire, from
exactly the same spot

right
Hereford cider label with
old bull

The Malvern Hills rise whale-like and unexpectedly above the Severn Plain, the precipitous streets of Great Malvern lined with Gothic villas peeping from behind laurel shrubberies like an upright Cheltenham. Up on the hills proper one can look out east over Worcestershire and see an orderly pattern of fields stretching towards Pershore, Evesham and the Cotswold escarpment. Church bells sounding out over the pink and white blossoms of fruit orchards, an English Arcadia.

But turn round and face west into Herefordshire. The contrast could not be more marked. The slope of the hill on this side is less distinct from the fields stretching into the blue distance. Here are fold upon fold of lesser hills crowned with trees, isolated farms at the heart of sheep pastures, cider orchards and soil as red as a Hereford bull. The sense of a more hidden, mysterious landscape, preparing us for Hay Bluff and the Welsh Borders.

Blaise Hamlet

Tucked away in north Bristol at Henbury is a tiny enclave that contains a microcosm of all that is eccentric and delightful about English buildings. In 1811 a Quaker banker asked architectural supremo John Nash to design an estate of cottages for his aged retainers in their retirement. From the pavement a set of steps goes up from a gap in a stone wall to where a path winds through the trees into Blaise Hamlet. You may start looking around for a White Rabbit with a pocket watch because this is surely Alice's Wonderland.

Blaise Hamlet comprises nine *cottage orné* dwellings around a greensward complete with sundialed village pump. Each cottage is unique, built in stone rubble in a variety of picturesque styles. Three are roofed in bountiful thatch, at least two appear to have dovecotes built into the gables. All have pronounced chimneys – made deliberately tall to accentuate the skyline – some round, some polygonal, some set diagonally to the roof ridge. How anybody can come here and not be moved by Blaise Hamlet is beyond me. But Pevsner thought it all very sentimental, remarking, 'Its progeny is legion and includes Christmas cards and teapots'. Quite good then.

Magpies and Ironworks

above
Original lifeboat station,
Wells-next-the-Sea,
Norfolk

bottom left
Stokesay Castle
Gatehouse, Shropshire

bottom right
Feathers Hotel, Ludlow,
Shropshire

The western counties bordering Wales are full of half-timbered buildings, the immensely popular 'magpie' cottages and houses that, unlike their eastern counterparts, prefer to emphasise the contrast between timber and plaster, to show how it all works by using black together with white, cream or yellow paint. One immediately thinks of the showpieces in Shropshire: the fairy-tale Jacobean gatehouse to Stokesay Castle; the fanciful Feathers Hotel in Ludlow, more artwork than architecture. Further north, Cheshire's Little Moreton Hall towers and leans into the breeze like a galleon robbed of sails.

But, I'd like to slip in here a vote for corrugated iron. Much maligned, particularly if it actually does go rusty and waves about in the wind, it is nevertheless a remarkable material that meant buildings could be put up quickly and cheaply. Henry Robinson Palmer is credited with inventing it in 1828, realising that corrugating sheets of iron increases its tensile strength, and galvanising the metal protects it from oxidising. It also lends itself admirably to

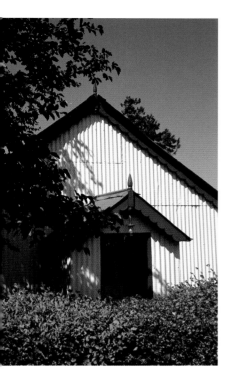

above
Corrugated-iron barn
manufacturer's sign

top left
Woodmancote Chapel,
Worcestershire

top right
Gunthorpe Marina on the
River Trent, Nottinghamshire

right
Red Gate Farm, Guyhirne,
Cambridgeshire

being painted in any shade on the colour chart. Farm buildings immediately come to mind, but the material has been used to prefabricate everything from village halls to complete houses. They are also possibly the only buildings where the erector leaves his name on a prominent plate.

Harrods had whole churches (tin tabernacles) in their catalogue and exported them in flat packs all over the Empire, complete with Gothic accessories like wooden porches and bellcotes. Mobile shepherds' huts began to be made of corrugated iron, costing £4 in 1930. If you can find a restored one for sale now you could be relieved of £8,000.

Because of its use as a thatch substitute and its make-do-and-mend properties it has certainly had its detractors, not least in the early days from architectural *über* critic Ruskin. The

surprise, though, is that it actually does fit in with the landscape, particularly as it gains a rich patina of earthy colour from its gradual deterioration. I'm a fan, and I have to tell you I'm not alone. There is even a Corrugated Iron Club, its members gently rippling with enthusiasm. How English is that?

Hardnott Pass, Cumbria

Hampshire from Beacon Hill

Bulwick, Northamptonshire

Blakeney, Norfolk

Hemingford Grey, Cambridgeshire

Port Isaac Bay, Cornwall

down Forest, East Sussex

Goodrich, Herefordshire

ves, North Yorkshire

Isle of Grain, Kent

at Postland Fen, Lincolnshire

Berry Head, Devon

above
Castle of Mystery,
Ridsdale, Northumberland

opposite
Cragside, Rothbury,
Northumberland

The North

The north of England is dominated and divided by the Pennines. The Yorkshire Dales with small fields edged by stone walls and owl-haunted barns. To the east, the run to the coast passing through villages of stone-built cottages with bright orange pantiled roofs. Lowland Lancashire villages with colourful renders and painted window surrounds hold their own against the urban sprawl of Manchester and Liverpool. It's impossible to do proper justice to the northern landscapes in such a limited space, and I've really only just started to get to grips with it. But I have stood up on the Hardnott Pass in Cumbria after a violent rain storm waiting for the sun to illuminate the fort, watching a bar of light widening as it crossed the sea far off to the west, the fields and woods below suddenly lighting up as it advanced towards me. Coming back down from these heights into Eskdale was like coming indoors.

Over in Northumberland I can't keep away from Norman Shaw's Cragside for long, built on a wild hillside above Rothbury for arms magnate Sir William Armstrong. Next to Waddon in Dorset I think this is the most satisfying house in England. The south elevation seems to embody everything I love about English building, with its extraordinary palette of colour and almost haphazard grouping of black and white timber-framing, creamy stone masonry and deep pink roof tiles. All of it framed by sombre green firs and shrubberies.

The last time I was up here I travelled from Rothbury across the broad empty backbone of England to Corbridge and came across what looked like a Border castle in the middle of a field at Ridsdale. I photographed it, got back in my car and headed south. Back home I rummaged through all my guidebooks, reference volumes, leaflets and scraps of paper; and comprehensively failed to find out anything about it all. *Unmitigated England* is like that, continually presenting us with new puzzles and old mysteries, always giving out reminders to help us discover something forgotten, amazing or just simply something very good to look at, whichever way the signpost points or the road takes us.

Cragside

Over a century of life on a Northumbrian hillside
Is preserved in Victorian glory for this day.
Through snow, rain and sun;
Through the sound of guns echoing on nearby moorland
And the crunch of limousine tyres on carefully raked gravel.
Through glass and silver suppers lit by Swan's first bulbs;
Watercolours, eggs and sightless birds mere backdrops
To cigar-smoked billiard room conversation.
Preserved 'til now on a windswept July morning
The past becomes clearer through the mist that hides
The detail of another life.
Peter Ashley

ESSENTIAL ENGLAND

Essential Reading

As you would expect, my bookshelves groan with books that have the word 'England' or 'English' in the title. Everybody will have their favourites, but this list is just a personal selection of books that have not only given me interesting and unique insights, but that have also given me great pleasure in the actual reading. It excludes the guidebooks to England that I have mentioned in the chapter Guidebook England.

Non-Fiction

Bates, H.E. (illustrated by Tunnicliffe, C.F.). *O More than Happy Countryman* (Country Life, 1943)

Bell, Adrian (illustrated by Nash, John). *Men and the Fields* (Batsford, 1939)

Betjeman, John, ed. *Collins Guide to English Parish Churches* (Collins, 1959)

Betjeman, John (Lycett Green, Candida, ed.). *Coming Home* (Methuen, 1997)

Betjeman, John. *First and Last Loves* (John Murray, 1969)

Clifton-Taylor, Alec and Ireson, A.S. *English Stone Building* (Gollancz, 1983)

Cook, Olive and Smith, Edwin. *English Cottages and Farmhouses* (Thames & Hudson, 1954)

Darley, Gillian. *Villages of Vision* (Paladin Granada, 1978)

Deakin, Roger. *Waterlogged* (Chatto & Windus, 1999)

Goldsmith Carter, George. *Forgotten Ports of England* (Evans, 1952)

Hoskins, W.G. *The Making of the English Landscape* (Hodder & Stoughton, 1955)

Ingrams, Richard, ed. (illustrated by O'Connor, John). *England An Anthology* (Collins, 1989)

Jenkins, Simon. *England's Thousand Best Churches* (Allen Lane, The Penguin Press, 1999)

Jenkins, Simon. *England's Thousand Best Houses* (Allen Lane, 2003)

Jennings, Paul and Gorham, John. *The English Difference* (Aurelia, 1974)

Lamb, Lynton. *County Town* (Eyre & Spottiswoode, 1950)

Lycett Green, Candida. *England: Travels Through An Unwrecked Landscape* (Pavilion, 1996)

Lycett Green, Candida. *Over the Hills and Far Away* (Doubleday, 2002)

Mabey, Richard. *Home Country* (Century, 1990)

Mabey, Richard. *Nature Cure* (Chatto & Windus, 2005)

Penoyre, John and Jane. *Houses in the Landscape* (Faber & Faber, 1978)

Piper, John. *Buildings and Prospects* (The Architectural Press, 1948)

Piper, John. *A Painter's Camera* (Tate Gallery, 1987)

Powers, Alan. *Eric Ravilious: Imagined Realities* (Imperial War Museum, 2004)

Priestley, J.B. *English Journey* (Heinemann Gollancz, 1934)

Russell, Ken. *Fire Over England* (Hutchinson, 1993)

Seymour, John. *Sailing Through England* (Eyre & Spottiswoode, 1956)

Simmons, Jack. *A Selective Guide to England* (John Bartholomew, 1979)

Sinclair, Iain. *Edge of the Orison* (Hamish Hamilton, 2005)

Thomas, Edward. *The Icknield Way* (Wildwood House, 1980)

Wilkinson, Philip and Ashley, Peter. *The English Buildings Book* (English Heritage, 2006)

Wright, Patrick. *The River, the Thames in Our Time* (BBC, 1999)

England: The Photographic Atlas (HarperCollins Illustrated, 2001)

I would also highly recommend the *Scrapbooks* produced by Robert Opie that show packaging and ephemera from the Victorian era to the 1980s, published by New Cavendish Books; and the West Country volumes by Peter W. Gray in the Ian Allan railway series which reproduce 35mm transparencies of trains, mostly taken between 1950 and 1970. Mr Gray stands out in this excellent series because his camera searches beyond the cliché of three-quarter view locomotives in order to capture the contemporary railway landscape.

Fiction

Bates, H.E. *A Moment in Time* (Michael Joseph, 1964)

Bates, H.E. *Seven by Five* (Michael Joseph, 1963)

Bates, H.E. (illustrated by Ardizzone, Edward). *My Uncle Silas* (Jonathan Cape, 1939)

Cowper Powys, John. *Wolf Solent* (Penguin Modern Classics, 1982)

Hartley, L.P. *The Go-Between* (Hamish Hamilton, 1953)

James, M.R. *Ghost Stories* (Penguin Popular Classics, 1994)

Jerome, Jerome K. *Three Men in a Boat* (Penguin Classics, 2004)

Lee, Laurie (illustrated by Ward, John). *Cider with Rosie* (Penguin, 1962)

Poetry

Betjeman, John.
Collected Poems (John Murray, 2003)
Summoned by Bells (John Murray, 1960)

Clare, John. *Selected Poems.* (Bate, John, ed., Faber & Faber, 2004)

Hardy, Thomas. *The Complete Poems* (Papermac, 1981)

Larkin, Philip. *Collected Poems* (The Marvell Press, Faber & Faber, 1988)

Thomas, Edward. *Collected Poems* (Faber & Faber, 2004)

Essential Places and Things

I would like everybody to be able to visit all the places and find the things mentioned in this book, and to enjoy them as I have done. Here's a small personal checklist of places and access points that I hope will be of use to the *Unmitigated England* explorer.

Marmite On Our Hovis There's really only one place to go: Robert Opie's *Museum of Brands Packaging and Advertising* (www.museumofbrands.com), which has finally found a good home in Colville Mews (off Lonsdale Road) in London's Notting Hill.

Songs Of Praise England is so rich in churches of all periods it is very difficult to produce a definitive essential list. But here's a handful: *Brixworth*, Northamptonshire; *Winterbourne Tomson*, Dorset; *Kilpeck*, Herefordshire; *Patrington*, East Yorkshire; *Northleach*, Gloucestershire; *Brookland*, Kent; *Blythburgh*, Suffolk; *Elsing*, Norfolk; *Staunton Harold*, Leicestershire. In London seek out *Hawksmoor's churches* as well as *Wren's* and for real surprises lose yourself in darkest Herefordshire for *Shobdon* and *Hoarwithy*. St Andrew's *Roker* in County Durham and *St Mary's*, *Wellingborough*, Northamptonshire are truly remarkable, hidden away in quiet side streets.

England On Film Most of the feature films I talked about are available on DVD. Also worth watching out for are the British Film Institute's series of vintage BBC films on DVD, which includes *A Warning to the Curious* and *Whistle and I'll Come to You*, classic adaptations of M.R. James ghost stories, set on the East Anglian coast (www.bfi.org.uk). A selection from the GPO Film Unit's films has been released as The GPO Classic Collection (www.moviemail-online.co.uk). Just about anything by Mr Betjeman passes muster, in particular *Metroland* and *A Passion for Churches*; and the *Talking Landscapes* series with Aubrey Manning is near perfect television. Look out too for showings at the National Film Theatre in London (website as BFI) and increasingly at the new little digital cinemas flickering into life at a village hall near you.

Guidebook England There's no substitute for rummaging about on the bowed shelves of a dusty second hand bookshop, but the website (www.abebooks.co.uk) will find you just about anything. I found Rex Wailes's classic book on English windmills in five seconds. In Massachusetts. Most country towns have at least one bookshop, probably with a notice on the door saying 'back in ten minutes', but if you want to be totally overwhelmed try *Barter Books* in Alnwick, Northumberland (www.barterbooks.co.uk). At least it's in an old railway station and has open fires in the winter. If you want books just to read, condition won't be important, but if you want to collect books always go for the best possible condition you can afford, always with the elusive dust jackets if they ever had them.

A Particular Kind Of Pub We're on dodgy territory here as discussed. If you're in London take a look at the *Mitre Tavern* in Ely Place, *The Grapes* in Narrow Street, Limehouse, the *Black Friar* in Queen Victoria Street, the *Cittie of Yorke* in High Holborn, the *Red Lion* in Duke of York Street and *The Clifton* in Clifton Hill, Maida Vale. One's never sure about committing pubs to any kind of list, such are today's vagaries of ownership. Is the *Drewe Arms* in Drewsteignton, Devon still as it was fifteen years ago? Or the *Masons Arms* in Branscombe, in the same county? I fear for the Compasses at Littley Green in Essex now that Ridley's brewery has gone from just down the lane. Safer bets are the *Crown* at Old Dalby in Leicestershire, the *Falcon* in Arncliffe, North Yorkshire, *The Bell* in Walberswick, Suffolk, the *Lord Nelson* in Burnham Thorpe, Norfolk and the tiled floor bar at the *Castle* in Chiddingstone, Kent. If you want a 1970s' *Life on Mars* experience lift the catch of *The Gate* in Bisbrooke, Rutland before it's too late.

Station To Station There have been some excellent restorations of railway stations that still serve our dwindling network of lines: *Hertford East*, *Grange-over-Sands*, *Market Harborough*, *Brighton* and *Manchester*'s glorious new glass and aluminium roof. But for the fire-bucket-and-porter's-trolley railway experience as described here we must visit the preserved steam lines of England. *The Bluebell Line* (www.bluebell-railway.co.uk) from Sheffield Park to Kingscote via Horsted Keynes in East Sussex was one of the first, the 20-mile *West Somerset Line* running under the Quantocks from Bishops Lydeard to Minehead is the longest (www.west-somerset-railway.co.uk). The *Severn Valley Railway* reinvents the GWR, from Bridgnorth in Shropshire to Kidderminster in Worcestershire (www.svr.co.uk). Apart from Santa and fireworks specials, the workings tend to be seasonal, but you can travel on the *Settle to Carlisle Line* at any time (www.settle-carlisle.co.uk).

The Open Road is difficult to find anywhere, but don't forget the *Milestone Society* (www.milestone-society.co.uk), and to see just how attractive motoring used to be a visit to the *National Motor Museum* at Beaulieu in Hampshire is really essential (www.beaulieu.co.uk). Here are serried ranks of cars, commercial vehicles and motorbikes alongside signs, accessories and motoring ephemera. The Shell Art Collection is housed here, and a small selection is on public display. Otherwise you could take a 1938 Wolseley out for a spin, park it in a field gateway and take twenty minutes to boil a kettle on a paraffin Primus stove.

England By The Sea If you want to see just how garish, colourful, noisy, dramatic, dyed-blonde and over-lipsticked an English seaside resort can be then get it all over with at just one resort: *Blackpool* (www.blackpool.com). Otherwise steer clear of the coastal conurbations and head for less-populated areas. The *National Trust* ('for ever, for everyone' is their catchphrase– which is nice) cares for over 700 miles of coastline in England, Wales and Northern Ireland, and their website has details of many coastal walks (www.nationaltrust.org.uk). Places that have a particularly English flavour for me include: *Aldeburgh* in Suffolk, *Deal* in Kent, *Hastings* and *Brighton* in Sussex, *Sidmouth* in Devon, *St Ives* and *Port Isaac* in Cornwall, *Clevedon* in Somerset and *Ravenglass* in Cumbria.

Shopkeepers' Shops Proper shops and shopkeepers need to be rediscovered, and that's half the fun. But far more importantly they need to be used, to have things bought regularly from them. The big supermarkets won't go away, but perhaps we should start to regard them more as warehouses for Brillo Pads and toilet paper and use local retailers who offer local produce and personal service. Support farmers' markets (www.farmersmarkets.net) and city markets like *Borough* in Southwark, London (www.boroughmarket.org.uk). One shop I know has got it absolutely right. *Old Town Clothing* is a little clothes emporium in Holt, Norfolk, and is what this book would be if it were a shop. Their website is also utterly brilliant (www.old-town.co.uk). Read particularly the piece called 'The Ploughman's Lunchbox'. Perfect.

Coloured Counties The West Country and the Lake District shouldn't be ignored, just given a rest now and then. These are the big set pieces that cause motorway jams every bank holiday, but off piste are unsung delights on little-used roads. The *Lincolnshire Wolds* with forgotten estates and tiny churches like *Oxcombe*, curious names like *Bag Enderby* and *Ashby Puerorum*. Or north Bedfordshire and the Ouse Valley, one of H.E. Bates's countries, with stone villages and medieval bridges at *Harrold* and *Oakley*. *East* (or *High*) *Leicestershire*, *Rutland* away from the reservoir, and northeast Northamptonshire villages like *Apethorpe* and *Deene*. *Gloucestershire* always repays getting off the beaten track, up in the north west corner around *Newent* and *Dymock* and out in the middle of the big Severn meander beyond *Frampton* and *Saul* at *Arlingham Passage*. Northumberland roads out to the west of *Rothbury*, country lanes on the *Plain of Holderness* to the east of Hull, *Kilnsea*, *Spurn Head* and back over the Humber Bridge to unvisited country north of Scunthorpe around *Alkborough*. *Corrugated-iron shepherds' huts* can be found at www.shepherdshuts.co.uk

A note on the type

Unmitigated England is typeset in two classic English typefaces. Gill for the headings and Baskerville for the text.

ACKNOWLEDGEMENTS

Acknowledgements

I have received much help, encouragement and support in producing *Unmitigated England*. I would particularly like to thank, in alphabetical order: Misha Anikst, Ben Ashley, George Ashley, Kathy Ashley, Wilfred Ashley, Christine Beckwith, Lucy Bland, Simon Bland, Jennie Browning, David Campbell, Coleman Group, Ptolemy Dean, Gee Farnsworth, Rupert Farnsworth, Richard Gregory, Frank Harper, Leigh Hooper, Alfonso Iacurci, Clémence Jacquinet, Stuart Kendall, Candida Lycett Green, Nigel Parker, Sarah Peacock, Dominic Owen, Biff Raven-Hill, Joyce Raven-Hill, Justin Savage, Margaret Shepherd, Greg Southwell, Karen Southwell, David Spain, David Stanhope, Christina Usher, James Warner, Philip Wilkinson, Colin Wise, Jo Wood

Illustrations

Most of the illustrations in this book are from the author's personal collections. Others have come from various sources, as listed below.

For the illustrations on the following pages the author and publisher would like to credit:

p.17   *Ovaltine Dairy Maid* © David Spain

p.53   'St George Reforne, Portland' by John Piper © Photo Tate Archive. John Piper Estate c/o Clarissa Lewis, Alltfadog Capel Madog, Aberystwyth, Ceredigion SY23 3JA, Wales, UK Tel: 01970 880 354

p.54   *The Go-Between* foyer card; p.59 *Went the Day Well* poster; p.65 *Far from the Madding Crowd* poster © Canal + Image UK Ltd

p.66   *Witchfinder General* DVD cover © Prism Leisure Corporation plc & Euro London Films Ltd

p.69   'Melton Constable Hall' © Edifice Picture Library

p.78   Shell lorry poster reproduced by kind permission of the Shell Art Collection and Bär & Karrer, Zurich

p.85   'Hidcote, Gloucestershire' © Edwin Smith / RIBA Library Photographs Collection

p.90   Illustration of beer glass by Barnett Freedman

p.105 Station Gate pub sign © The Sign Company

p.109 Image of ramblers from *150 Miles of Footpath Rambles Around Leicester*, Blackfriars Press (1936)

p.120 'Butlin's for Holidays' poster © National Railway Museum / Science & Society Picture Library

pp.138–139 Ordnance Survey Maps © Crown Copyright Ordnance Survey

p.161 *Cornish Riviera Express* by Galbraith O'Leary, from British Trains, Juvenile Productions Ltd, London (c. 1950)

Text

For permission to reprint copyright material the author and publisher gratefully acknowledge the following:

Title Page Extract from 'Great Central Railway Sheffield Victoria to Banbury' by John Betjeman © The Estate of John Betjeman. Reproduced by kind permission of John Murray (Publishers) Ltd

p.16   Extract from 'The Wykehamist' by John Betjeman © The Estate of John Betjeman. Reproduced by kind permission of John Murray (Publishers) Ltd

p.34   Extract from 'Pot Pourri from a Surrey Garden' by John Betjeman © The Estate of John Betjeman. Reproduced by kind permission of John Murray (Publishers) Ltd

p.44   Extract from *O More Than Happy Countryman* by H.E. Bates, published by Country Life (1943). Reprinted by kind permission of Country Life.

p.51   Extract from *Arts and Crafts Architecture* by Peter Davey, published by Phaidon Press © 1995 Phaidon Press Limited

p.68   Extract from *The Go-Between* by L.P. Hartley, published by Hamish Hamilton (1953). Copyright © L.P. Hartley, 1953. Reproduced by kind permission of Penguin Books Ltd.

p.74   Extract from *In Search of England* by H.V. Morton, published by Methuen Publishing Ltd (1933). Copyright © Marion Wasdell and Brian de Villiers

p.74   Extract from *The English: A Portrait of a People* by Jeremy Paxman, published by Michael Joseph (1998). Reproduced by kind permission.

p.85   Comment by John Betjeman on his resignation from the Shell Guides from *Piper's Places* by Richard Ingrams and John Piper, published by Chatto & Windus. Reprinted by permission of The Random House Group Ltd.

p.186 Extract from 'A Shropshire Lad' by A.E. Housman. Reprinted by kind permission of The Society of Authors, as the Literary Estate of A.E. Housman.

Every reasonable effort has been made to contact copyright holders of material reproduced in this book. Any omissions are entirely unintentional and should be notified to the publisher, who would be glad to hear from them and will ensure corrections are included in any reprints.

INDEX